Contents

C000094706

"Yet, in a hundred scenes, all much the same,

I know that weekly half a million men

Who never actually played the game,

Hustling like cattle herded in a pen,

Look on and shout,

While two-and-twenty hirelings hack a ball about."

Sir Owen Seaman (1861-1936)

(Surely not the great grandfather of the pony-tailed one)

They say that it is every young boy's dream to play professional football – something of an exaggeration, I fear. I still can't quite imagine the young Wayne Sleep drifting off into the night amid thoughts of lifting the FA Cup. Personally, I'd have given my right leg to play League football – well, perhaps not the leg. But it would have been a dream come true. Unfortunately, I was never able to realise my dream, just like the overwhelming majority of boys – and now girls – who ever kicked a football. And that is what makes the subjects of this book so special. Every one of them has achieved something that has proved beyond so many others.

Some of the players on these pages forged long and occasionally lucrative careers. Some have achieved international stardom and major domestic honours. Others have made but fleeting appearances in The League, sometimes as amateurs or part-timers. But whether they made three hundred appearances in The Premiership or appeared for only half a game in the Third Division, each has felt the thrill of crossing the touch-line to represent a club playing in the world's oldest professional league. And each has been the subject of expectation for thousands of fans desperate to be supporters of a successful team.

The inspiration for the book was close to home, my dad, Ken Chaytor having played for Oldham Athletic in the 1950's. It just seemed so fantastic when I was young knowing that he'd been a pro and I've been captivated by the notion of playing League football ever since.

There are only two criteria for inclusion. Firstly the player must have been born in the Borough of Sedgefield and secondly, they must have played in at least one Football League or Premiership match between the 1946/47 and 2000/01 seasons – between the war and the millennium. Now, it's important to say that the information in the book is based on the Premiership and Football League's own records, interviews with those who were willing and able to co-operate plus a certain amount of desk research. The memories of players are recorded and presented as facts or opinion in good faith. No doubt there will be one or two things of which people will have a different recollection. Place of birth is identified by the League records and there will be players who you thought were born in the district but in fact weren't, hence their non-inclusion. The opposite will also apply. As they say, 'that's football'. Any complaints should be addressed to Points of view, BBC Television and if enough people buy the book, I'll correct them in the second edition.

Finally, the Mad Ramblings are some of my own thoughts and opinions plus a few odd facts and co-incidences. There may be occasions when you wonder what the hell I'm on about but read it again and you'll know it makes sense.

So there you are. I got my retaliation in first. However, if you enjoy reading the result as much as I enjoyed writing and researching it – then you have my deepest sympathy because you too are probably obsessed by football.

Key to the statistics

The name will be followed by a letter denoting the player's regular position – (G) goalkeeper, (D) defender, (F) forward, (RH) right half, (CH) centre half, (LH) left half, (WH) wing half, (FB) full back, (IF) inside forward, (M) midfield, (OR) outside right, (LB) left back, (RB) right back, (OL) outside left, (OR) outside right, (CF) centre forward.

Below the name will be the place of birth followed by date of birth and in some cases the year of death. Any representative honours will be identified next and are self-explanatory.

Teams played for will be followed by seasons played, total number of League appearances including as substitute and number of goals scored. The source denotes the manner in which the player arrived at the club. When identifying seasons played the year denotes the first year of a season eg. 1970 means the 70/71 season. The key to the source is as follows: TR – transferred from the preceding team on the list. APP – apprentice player. L- denotes a loan period. YT – is a youth trainee. JNR – taken on as a junior. Where a club is named, that was the previous club.

The Nag's Head

8 West End, Sedgefield, Co. Durham TS21 2BS

Tel. 01740 620234

A Well Balanced Selection Of
Home Cooked Food
Served Throughout The Week

Traditional Sunday Lunches
Served 12 - 2.30 pm

Early Evening Specials
Served 5 - 7 pm

Our Restaurant / Function Room
is Available for Use
Throughout The Week

A Good Selection of
Fine Ales and Lagers

Up to *Five Real Ales* available

All served in a
Warm Family Atmosphere

The 'A' Team

	Seasons	apps	goals	source
Kevin Alderson (W) Shildon, 21 August 1953				
Darlington	1970	1	0	APP

Interviewed November 1999

Kevin Alderson is a Manchester Utd fan and proud of it, although he is subject to all the predictable jibes suffered by any United fan not born within a hundred yards of a cotton mill. His favourite players are Ryan Giggs and David Beckham. Both direct, attacking wingers who excite crowds and torment defences.

Darlington's Kevin "The Mighty Midget" Alderson in 1969

It is perhaps no surprise that he is drawn to this type of player since this is how he always tried to play the game himself. However, in three years as an apprentice at Darlington, he was only afforded one opportunity to excite the crowds in League football, appearing in the 2-0 win at York in 1970. Kevin was a nippy wingman who liked to get to the by-line and supply the central strikers but he believes that his own lack of ambition and lack of height (5 feet 3 inches but who's counting?) contributed in equal measure to his not forging a long-term career. He was taken on by Ray Yeoman as a fifteen-year-old and his trainer at the time was Chris Harker, the man who as goalkeeper for Bury collided with Brian Clough in 1962 bringing to a shattering, premature end the career of one of the greatest goal-scorers of all time. He made plenty of reserve team appearances and a number of minor first team outings but couldn't force his way into the regular first eleven. He was eventually released by Len Ritchley and played three trial matches as an under-19 at Blackpool, also being called up by the England youth squad to train at Bisham Abbey with the likes of David Armstrong, Kevin Beattie and Mervyn Day. However, an ankle injury dampened his spirits and he didn't return to Blackpool. Indeed, after playing for Tow Law for one season he turned his back on football as a potential profession and returned to the local leagues and a living away from the game.

He's worked at Flymo in Newton Aycliffe for the past fifteen years and doesn't bother much with football either as a player or a spectator. Although he has been enticed to turn out for the over-40's on the odd occasion, watching Man U on the box is still his greatest football interest.

Finally, Kevin can boast an interesting encounter with one of the century's true football heroes. Whilst killing time in the big-match build-up before United took on Brighton in the 1983 FA Cup Final, who should he bump into in a London betting shop but George Best? Apparently, Georgie was totally sober and perfectly charming but had no intention of going to the match.

	Seasons	apps	goals	source
Graeme Aldred (D) Ferryhill, 11 Sept 1966 Died 1987 Darlington	1984-85	44	1	Newc. Utd (YT)

Father interviewed November 1999

As a promising Bishop Auckland District and Durham County schoolboy, Graeme Aldred was spotted and taken on by Newcastle Utd when Brian Tinnion, Ian Bogie, Joe Allon and a certain Paul Gascoigne were all youth trainees at St. James'. As a teenager he had been trained by his father Colin, a former Northern League performer, doing relentless shuttle-runs and sprints to build up both speed and stamina. The young Aldred was a fierce competitor, a bad loser but a great trainer. Colin Suggett was the man entrusted with the progress of the Newcastle likely lads at a time when the first team boasted the talents of Kevin Keegan and Peter Beardsley. Indeed, Graeme was Beardsley's boot boy.

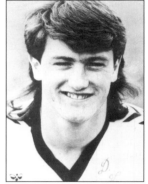

Graeme Aldred – Gone too soon

However, after two years rubbing shoulders with some of the biggest names in the modern game he was released by the recently appointed Jack Charlton and snapped up on his eighteenth birthday by Cyril Knowles at Darlington. His debut came four days later in a 0-0 draw at Bloomfield Road, Blackpool. 1984-85 turned into a highly successful season for The Quakers with promotion to the Third Division and a run to the fourth round of the FA Cup. The highlight of Graeme's career came in the third round when Darlington were David to Middlesbrough's Goliath and dumped their Second Division neighbours out of the Cup. The 2-1 replay victory at Feethams followed a 0-0 encounter at Ayresome Park with the crowds of 19,000 and 14,000 two of the biggest seen by Darlington fans in recent times. It was followed by one of the biggest disappointments of recent times, the fourth round 0-3 defeat at non-league Telford United after an initial 1-1 draw at Feethams. Graeme's one League goal came this season on 29th October in the 4-3 win at Aldershot.

His two years at Darlington were eventful and exciting and manager Knowles gained respect for his team building and man-management. He worked hard and nurtured his young talent but many people believe he made a mistake in letting too many of them leave in the 1986 close season. Graeme Aldred was amongst them. He moved to Whitley Bay where he soon earned a reputation as a star performer in non-league football and once again began to attract the attentions of League clubs. In a final, cruel twist of fate Phil Neal, the Bolton manager called to inquire about Graeme's availability the day before he died in a motoring accident. The one consolation was that his talents had not been forgotten.

	Seasons	apps	goals	source
Dale Anderson (F) Newton Aycliffe, 23 Aug 1970 Darlington	1986-88	15	0	YT
Middlesbrough	1990	0	0	TR

Interviewed August 1999

Dale Anderson may have only played in fifteen League games for Darlington but he had a long association with the club as a junior, apprentice and professional. It was also a highly eventful period in The Quakers' history with relegation from the Football League to the Vauxhall Conference in 1988-89 and immediate promotion back into the Fourth Division the following year on a tide of emotion and hope for a brighter future. During this period, Dale became the youngest player ever to appear in a League game for Darlington when he played in a Third Division fixture at Chesterfield aged 16 years and 254 days whilst still an apprentice. His manager then was Cyril Knowles who had been forced into blooding young talent because of a shortage of funds for experienced players.

Dale Anderson doing a passable impression of Shakin' Stevens in front of a Stockport defender in 1988.
(Photo: Darlington FC)

Dale was a full-time professional for two years from 1988-1990 signing for Dave Booth in the season Darlington fell from The League and spending his second year as a pro' in The Conference. A back injury and glandular fever restricted his appearances to a mere handful and he had to sit out most of this highly charged season as a spectator. He did, however, have the pleasure of working for Brian Little whom he describes as 'a brilliant boss'. He looked after his players, speaking straight when necessary but quick to praise. His method was quiet but strong and players were eager to impress and perform for him. The Quakers bounced straight back into The League but Dale didn't receive a medal because of his low tally of appearances. Nevertheless, he had shared in a great experience.

In the close season he signed for Middlesbrough and Colin Todd in a swap deal valued at £30,000, which took Michael Trotter to Darlington. However, more bad luck with injury, a gashed knee versus Bradford reserves, limited his chances and he eventually returned to play reserve team football at Darlington. Non-contract spells at Wycombe Wanderers and Port Vale proved unsuccessful and eventually Dale settled for an extension to his football career playing non-league. Three years at Bishop Auckland from 1993-96 were followed by a season with King's Lynn under the ex-Aston Villa, Manchester Utd and England full-back, John Gidman. He finally bowed out after a season with Evenwood in 1998.

Dale's best memory was beating Oldham Athletic 2-0 at Feethams in the first leg of a Littlewoods Cup tie. They eventually went out after extra time in the second leg against a team containing Dennis Irwin and Andy Ritchie amongst others. As the Oldham team was embarking on the most successful period in their history this was no small achievement by Darlington. He also recalls with delight partnering David Currie up front on his debut. Currie was a god at Feethams and a great natural talent who entertained fans at Middlesbrough, Barnsley, Nottingham Forest and Carlisle amongst others. David Ginola is his current favourite, 'the best I've ever seen' and one of that rare breed of players who runs directly at defences. It is Dale Anderson's view that this is how football should be played. I agree.

He doesn't watch Darlington now preferring the racetrack to the football stadium but he fervently hopes that George Reynolds' millions can move the club into a higher orbit. As for Dale, he's been a postman in Newton Aycliffe since 1995 and is very happy, thankyou.

A is for Aldrovandi Palace

The flight path of arrivals into Rome's Leonardo de Vinci airport takes the lucky traveller directly above The Eternal City. The view is of the majestic Tiber bordered by the grandeur of The Vatican, the magnificent decay of The Colosseum, the virtual reality of The Forum and most impressively for any football fan, The Stadio Olympico. This is the home of Lazio and Roma, two of the biggest teams in Europe and once host to the wanton talents of Gazza.

Now I'm not exactly Alan Whicker but I know a good hotel when I see one and The Aldrovandi Palace, on the north side of the intimidatingly huge Borghesi Gardens, is good. You know the sort of thing; chocolates on the pillow, showroom furniture and curtains so heavy and luxuriant it is a two man job to open them. There is origami toilet roll and a maid service, which is so frequent that you think you've brought another person on holiday with you. There's a weather forecast placed on your bedside table every morning, proper porters with uniforms who insist on carrying your bags everywhere and a breakfast room with so much fruit that you feel obliged to eat some.

Of course, such cosmopolitan places employ multi-lingual staff who make most English travellers feel decidedly inferior. However, it did enable me to enquire about the possibility of seeing the Roma or Lazio players in pre-season training. No chance Signor, they're in the Dolomites doing a spot of altitude work away from the glare of cameras and the distractions and temptations of everyday life.

This got me thinking about the lads back home working off a summer of excess on some wet and windy training ground before the Premiership kick off or playing out some utterly pointless pre-season tournament which serves only to satisfy sponsors or shareholders. Alright, attitudes and methods have changed significantly in this country but talk of the Dolomites did make me suspect that it is no wonder we fell so far behind the Europeans over the past thirty years.

Anyway, as I slopped around Rome in my trendy leather sandals it occurred to me that I looked like a centurion from the ankle downwards. And we did a fair amount of route marching up and down the most inspirational streets and piazzas from one wondrous ancient ruin to another. All very hard on my left achilles tendon you understand. This is the tendon I snapped while playing 7 a-side football in Middlesbrough in 1992, an injury which cruelly curtailed a promising career and worse still, left me with a skinny leg. I recall my consultant at the time informing me that his colleague in Liverpool had treated John Barnes for a similar injury, only he had received more sophisticated treatment and an operation while my tendon had effectively been shoved back together to get me walking again. Just the sort of thing I didn't want to hear really.

Nevertheless, Rome was mesmerising and the Aldrovandi Palace a treat, though I never did get to see any footballers apart from some utterly pointless pre-season tournament on Eurosport.

The 'B' Team

	Seasons	apps	goals	source
Frederick Barber (G)				
Ferryhill, 26 August 1963				
Darlington	1982-85	135	0	APP
Everton	1986	0	0	TR
Walsall	1986-90	153	0	TR
Peterborough Utd	1989	6	0	L
Chester City	1990	3	0	L
Blackpool	1990	2	0	L
Chester City	1990	5	0	L
Peterborough Utd	1991-94	63	0	TR
Colchester Utd	1992	10	0	L
Luton Town	1994	0	0	TR
Peterborough Utd	1994	5	0	L
Ipswich Town	1995	1	0	L
Blackpool	1995	1	0	L
Birmingham City	1995	1	0	TR

Interviewed June 1999

Perhaps Fred Barber was just born to be a goalkeeper. He did it at school, he did it in the Football League for 13 years and now he shows other people how to do it with the Puma Goalkeeping School, the country's first specialist coaching company for 'keepers. He and colleague Malcolm Webster, another ex-goalie, formed the company to run a series of residentials, summer schools and night schools which includes coaching professionals in the pre-season to help them to 'hit the ground running' when a new campaign starts. He rates Richard Wright as the best of the new breed he has worked with and tips him as a future England player. But ask him who was the best he's seen and Neville Southall is the name on his lips. Fred understudied Southall at Everton in 1986 when he was substitute for the Charity Shield at Wembley. He never got to appear in The League for them but did feature in a pre-season tour when Southall was injured and amongst others, he played against Ruud Gullit at Feyenoord.

Everton's new goalie, Fred Barber in 1986, unaware that as he poses for a picture the crowd has sneaked out of the stadium

His move to Everton from Darlington was somewhat ironic. Representatives from Merseyside had watched Darlington play a draw against Telford in the FA Cup and liked what they saw. They made an offer for Fred who was reluctant to leave his beloved Darlington but was persuaded by assistant manager, John Craggs to take his chance. Craggs drove him to Everton personally where he signed for his new club who were then drawn in the next round of The Cup against Telford who had beaten Darlington in the replay.

Fred had enjoyed four happy seasons at Feethams where he replaced Pat Cuff in goal and won promotion to the Third Division under Cyril Knowles. However, it was Martin Burleigh, another well travelled 'keeper who was his greatest early mentor. He had once asked Fred which of them was the better goalkeeper and Fred had replied that Burleigh was. Burleigh reacted by slapping him around the face and telling him never to forget that he was the best. Self-belief is everything for a 'keeper.

After his brief flirtation with the high life at Everton, Fred was snapped up by Walsall manager, Tommy Coakley to replace his good friend Mark Prudhoe. The Fellows Park outfit won plaudits for their attacking style and also won promotion to the Second Division in 1987, beating Bristol City 4-0 in the play-offs. A series of loans in 1989 and 1990 preceded a permanent move to Peterborough Utd in 1991 where he worked under Chris Turner and won another play-off versus Stockport. Finally playing at Wembley was a dream come true for Fred who described the adrenalin pumping experience thus:

" Imagine the best thing in the world that could happen to you. This was four times as quick and four times as good."

He experienced Wembley again in 1999 as the goalkeeping coach to the defeated Bolton side attempting to regain their Premiership status. However, he could only watch helplessly as the Bolton players slipped away in absolute dejection and he moved on to his next coaching assignment.

Fred's playing career was effectively ended by a shattering injury whilst at Peterborough which saw him stretchered unconscious from the pitch amid fears that he'd broken his neck. As it turned out, it was a severe shoulder break that required pioneering surgery to correct. He still has the plate and hook in the shoulder but claims that the injury may have been a blessing in disguise since it allowed him to take his first steps into coaching. Several short-term moves followed and he played his last League game under Barry Fry at Birmingham City. But now it's coaching all the way. As I spoke to him he'd just been invited to Toronto to run a course for Canadian 'keepers and there's still plenty of work at home. Management holds no appeal because your destiny is not always in your own hands but coaching goalkeepers in the English Leagues offers Fred the chance to unearth and develop some home-grown talent to match the flood of overseas 'keepers currently on show.

	Seasons	apps	goals	source
Arthur Bell (RH)				
Sedgefield, 5 March 1931				
Barrow	1950	1	0	Hylton Colliery

Arthur Bell's one and only League appearance came in the 1950/51 season as Barrow struggled near the bottom of the Third Division (North). The Sedgefield born right-half was signed in the August just before the campaign began by Barrow's longest serving manager, Jack Hacking, himself capped three times as England goalkeeper in 1929 whilst playing for Second Division Oldham Athletic. After his brief flirtation with the Football League, Arthur returned to the Sunderland area to continue a non-league career.

	Seasons	apps	goals	source
Laurence Brown (CH)				
Shildon, 22 August 1937				
Died 1998 E Amat				
Darlington (Am)	1958	3	0	Bishop Auckland
Northampton Town	1960	33	22	Bishop Auckland
Arsenal	1961-63	101	2	TR
Tottenham Hotspur	1963-65	62	3	TR
Norwich City	1966-68	81	2	TR
Bradford Park Avenue	1968-69	36	1	TR

Interviewed widow July 1999

Born and raised in Shildon, Laurie Brown was a talented junior boxing champion before turning to football. He had left school at fifteen to become an apprentice shop-fitter and cabinet-maker but national service took him south where he joined Woking on amateur terms. However, it soon became clear that he should be performing on a bigger stage and the offers came in thick and fast but for Laurie turning professional was something he was quite prepared to delay until he fulfilled another ambition. He had been on Fulham's books after being spotted at Woking but never made the first team. He returned north to resume an amateur playing career with Bishop Auckland taking a brief interlude at Darlington with three appearances in 1958. As an English amateur international he was selected to represent Great Britain at the Olympic Games in Rome, 1960. He therefore waited until after becoming an Olympian before signing professional forms for Northampton in 1960 where in his only season as a striker he was moved to centre-forward and topped the scoring list with 22 in 33 games.

Laurie Brown in a very tight Tottenham shirt in 1965.
(Photo: A. Wilkes and Son)

His talents were recognised by Arsenal manager George Swindin who took him to Highbury in August 1961 for a fee of £30,000 in the same year that Dennis Law left Manchester City for Torino in a then British record deal of £99,999. His move to Tottenham for £45,000 in 1963 was greeted with anger by the Gunners' fans who gave him a torrid time when the teams met that season. However, Laurie had the honour of playing under the great Bill Nicholson and with two of his idols, Dave Mackay and Jimmy Greaves as well as becoming a great friend of Pat Jennings, so he soon felt at home at White Hart Lane. After five seasons at the highest level of the English game, never out of the top half of the table, Laurie moved to Norwich City of the Second Division. He put in two solid seasons before his League career ended as player-manager at Bradford where Park Avenue finished bottom of the Fourth Division. They would do the same thing the next year and be replaced in the League by Cambridge Utd in the annual re-election drama. Spells as player-manager at Kings Lynn and Altrincham followed in the early 1970's before the Browns moved back to the North -East.

Laurie and his wife spent two years managing the Redworth Arms in Shildon before he started driving milk tankers for a living. Margaret could never stand the smokey atmosphere in the pub. She does, however, recall fondly the atmosphere of the Spennymoor Rink where she and Laurie first met doing the jive and dancing to the earliest rock 'n' roll. He was apparently pretty nifty on the dance floor as well as being an all-round sportsman. They were engaged while he was at Northampton and had their twin children whilst at Arsenal. Laurie junior is still a mad keen

Gunners' fan. One of Laurie's only regrets was turning down the opportunity to take on the player-manager's role at Bury after his spell at Bradford. This could have been a springboard to an extended career as a League manager. However, he had no regrets about a playing career in which he was idolised at Northampton and Norwich, rubbed shoulders with the greats at Arsenal and Tottenham and represented his country at the Olympic Games. Not a bad C.V.

	Seasons	apps	goals	source
Joseph Brunskill (F)				
Carlton, 22 April 1932				
Died 1989				
Sunderland	1950	0	0	Newc. Utd (Am)
Oldham Athletic	1954	12	2	TR

Joe Brunskill was a big man, a religious man and an impressive footballer who had always dreamed of playing for Sunderland. Although at 18 he was coveted by a number of top clubs, he stuck to his aim of trying to succeed at Roker Park when they were known as the 'Bank of England club'. He never quite made it at Sunderland and was eventually lured to Oldham by Owen Willoughby who had attracted a number of players from the area to Boundary Park. Joe made an immediate impact for the Latics scoring on his debut in a 2-2 draw at Barnsley in the Third Division (North). But the success was short-lived and he was replaced at centre-forward in October by Don Travis, a prolific scorer at Accrington Stanley, Crewe and Chester. Joe never regained a regular place in the team and left the club at the end of the season. Some believe that he wasn't ruthless enough to match his ability and make it big on the field. However, he had a keen eye for a talented player and became a respected scout for, amongst others, Queens Park Rangers and Manchester Utd. Indeed, such was his standing at Old Trafford that, following his sudden death in 1989, Brian Kidd and Alex Ferguson attended his funeral in his home town of Shildon and United paid for all the funeral arrangements. He had been attending a tournament in Whitley Bay and had taken ill while looking out for young talent. A fitting finale, perhaps, for a man who was so thoroughly immersed in football.

	Seasons	apps	goals	source
Thomas 'Billy' Bushby (CF)				
Shildon, 21 August 1914				
Died 1998				
Southend Utd	1934-38	40	13	Wolves (Am)
Portsmouth	1939	0	0	TR
Southampton	1946	2	0	TR

Billy Bushby was another product of the Shildon Colliery Wefare who made all but two of his League appearances before the Second World War. After a short spell with First Division Wolves in 1933-34, he was signed by Southend United of the Third Division (South). His new manager was the ex Arsenal and England goal-scorer, David Jack whose period in charge at Roots Hall was marked by an almost constant struggle to stay in business. Indeed, such was the lack of resources at smaller clubs Jack was identified on team photographs of the time as Mr. David Jack, Secretary-Manager. Although his first team appearances were limited to forty in five seasons, Billy scored a creditable thirteen League goals before Hitler so rudely interrupted. Aged twenty-five at the outbreak of war, Billy Bushby was deprived of the six years that would have represented his footballing prime. On the resumption of League football in 1946, he had moved south and played out his final two League matches at The Dell with Second Division Southampton. At thirty-five his League career was over and he transferred to Cowes on the Isle of Wight. He remained resident on the south coast until his death in 1998.

B is for Birthday

.....mine to be precise; the 24th May 1960. This is of concern to about six people in the whole world. However, there are others born on the same date but different years in whom rather more interest is guaranteed. There's Bob Dylan, decent singer, 1941. There's Victoria, useful queen, 1819. Then there's Eric Cantona, genius footballer, 1966.

Now everyone has an opinion about Cantona and particularly the infamous flying tackle on the Crystal Palace fan. I for one believe there was a certain honour in his actions. After all, if a drunken slob hurled foul abuse at you and insulted your mother in front of a crowd of onlookers, wouldn't you feel inclined to respond accordingly? If only the stewards, police or so-called decent fans had done something, Cantonna would not have been called into action. Of course, the most amusing part of the whole affair was the reaction of one affronted Palace supporter who threw his cup of tea over the Frenchman in disgust. How quaint; how quintessentially English. That'll teach Johnny Foreigner.

But 24th May was also the day that one of the twentieth century's greatest politicians died. Harold Wilson shuffled off in 1995 having suffered from Alzheimer's disease for several years. A cruel end for such a brilliant mind. He won four general elections, held together a feuding Labour Party and bequeathed to the nation the great Open University. But the thing I most admired about Harold was his home in St. Mary's on the Scilly Isles. I stumbled upon it whilst on holiday there in 1980. A totally unremarkable bungalow on a gently sloping street leading away from the town centre from where

Harold and the family walked, went bird watching and enjoyed the peace and solitude Prime Ministers must crave. Fittingly modest for a socialist leader. Shame about the other two homes.

As a Huddersfield boy, Harold was a big fan of the Town team of the Herbert Chapman era, League Champions three times in a row from 1923-4 to 1925-6. Leeds Road was the scene of many great triumphs in that pre-war period and it also proved to be one of my earliest footballing memories. The old red brick façade was perched just off the Manchester to Leeds road like a row of terraced houses and seemed to symbolize football at the heart of a community. As we motored past on the way to see relatives in Oldham, tuned in to Jimmy Clitheroe on the radio, I would crane my neck to get a glimpse of the signs over the turnstile gates and imagine people heaving through them on a match day to watch real professionals in a real stadium.

Of course, Leeds Road is long departed to be replaced by the spaceship that is the Macalpine Stadium with its shockingly good facilities and customer focus. I shouldn't complain since this is part of the modernisation of British football that had to happen and has probably done much to save the game from decay and demise. And even though the new developments have destroyed a little of the romance, they have been accompanied by a decline in the sort of behaviour, which caused Eric Cantona to get so upset. And it's nice to be able to go to the toilet without getting your feet wet.

The 'C' Team

	Seasons	apps	goals		source
James Cain (WH)					
Fishburn, 29 December 1933					
Bradford Park Avenue	1955	1	0		Ferryhill
Bristol City	1957	0	0	•	Stockton
Hartlepool Utd	1960-61	30	0		South Shields

Interviewed September 2001

Consider the following day of work - then ask yourself if Ravanelli would do it. Rise at 5.00am and have a hearty breakfast. Get your kit together for a 6.00am shift down the pit and march off to work. You're a fitter and today you're working on a cutter at the coal-face - all day. At the shift changeover you head off to ride the loco three miles back to the shaft - but you miss the train. You then run the three miles up the tunnel in your pit boots and are raised to the surface by 5.00pm. Run home, kick off your boots and grab your football gear. Cadge a lift on your mate's motorbike and roar off to Hartlepool's Victoria Ground. Arrive at the ground at 5.50pm for a 6.00pm kick-off and get a bollocking for being late. Take the field and have one of your best games for the club. After the match, accept the plaudits of your manager who thinks you must have had a restful day to have played so well. Alright, it didn't happen every home game but it did happen once to Jimmy Cain.

Jimmy Cain making a subtle challenge for South Shields in 1955

In all his years playing football, whether League or non-league, he never gave up the day job. He'd had plenty of offers to go full-time but, in common with many others at that time, decided that he was better off playing part-time whilst retaining another job. A fitter's apprenticeship at Fishburn after leaving school at fifteen was his chosen route and it was a career that would see him through to retirement. In contrast to this stability, he moved from club to club as a footballer and 'had more trials than a judge'. As a schoolboy, he clearly showed immense promise and was whetting the appetite of numerous League outfits, most notably Manchester United. In fact Matt Busby and Jimmy Murphy came to Fishburn to see him but his mother wouldn't let them in. Jimmy was getting a trade and that was the end of it. His mother always claimed that she saved him from being killed in the Munich air crash.

Broom juniors and Winterton were his first teams followed by stints at Blackhall in the North-Eastern League, Whitby and Ferryhill. However, it was a chance decision to sign for Trimdon Grange one spare Saturday that took his career to another level. He liked the club so much he stayed and they reached the final of the Sunderland Ship Owners Cup at Roker Park. They lost to Sunderland reserves but when Jimmy was soaking his sorrows in the bath he was approached by Jimmy Seed. The chief scout for Bristol City offered Jim the chance of professional football on the strength of his performance. He was persuaded to go on tour to Dublin and signed for Bristol City in 1957 on the promise of a job in the coal industry when he moved. No job materialized, so Jimmy left the West Country in the close season and returned to his old position at Fishburn. It was at Bristol he encountered centre-forward and England international, Johnny Atyeo, the best player he ever turned out with. It was also his biggest regret that things didn't work out at Ashton Gate. After eventually being released from his contract, he signed for South Shields where he enjoyed his favourite football moment when they beat Crewe Alexander 5-0 in an FA Cup first round replay only to lose 0-2 to Oldham in round two. He spent three happy seasons on Tyneside before ex-Hartlepool winger, Tommy McGuigan, also playing at Shields, offered to fix him up at The Victoria Ground. He was true to his word and Jimmy signed for manager Bill Robinson in August 1960. He went on to play in thirty Fourth Division games for the 'Pools and was also a member of the team who played out Hartlepool's first ever League Cup tie, a 1-2 defeat at the hands of Oldham Athletic at Boundary Park.

His League debut did not come for Hartlepool though. Two years earlier in 1955 and still with Ferryhill, he was tempted down to Bradford Park Avenue by old friend Gordon Bradley. The team was struggling near the foot of Third Division (North) and was without a manager. The chairman agreed to the signing as an amateur and Jimmy made his League bow versus Wrexham. Soon afterwards, Arthur Corkhill signed as player/manager and wanted Jimmy to play full-time. This wasn't in the Cain script so he left Bradford after one appearance and returned to Ferryhill.

Following his release from Hartlepool in 1962 - he actually got a better offer from Blyth Spartans - his football career continued non-league. He was offered a job and an extension to his playing career in Canada by Owen Willoughby who had at one time taken Jimmy on trial at Oldham. However, the home bird remained where he was, continuing in the mining industry and staying involved in football through coaching, scouting and supporting Middlesbrough. He still lives in Sedgefield but is much happier since he gave up his season ticket at The Riverside.

	Seasons	apps	goals	source
Peter Carr (FB)				
Bishop Middleham, 25 August 1951				
Darlington	1967-72	135	1	APP
Carlisle Utd	1972-77	204	1	TR
Hartlepool Utd	1979	22	0	New England (USA)

Interviewed August 2001

As we speak, Peter Carr is quite probably doing the daily checks on the pool at his Cape Cod motel in Massachusetts on the wild and wonderful North Atlantic coast of America. Or perhaps he's nipped down to Nantucket where the millionaires are being driven out by the locals - the billionaires. For over twenty years this has been his home and his living. As he puts it, he has "...a great life in God's country". And it's football that made it all possible.

Born in Bishop Middleham but brought up largely by his grand parents in Ferryhill, he went to the local primary and then to Chilton secondary modern along with his good friend, Ian Larnach who also went on to play League football. He had been courted by numerous clubs but was finally signed as an apprentice by Darlington and made his League debut in the last game of the 1967/68 season in a 0-0 draw at Exeter. He was just 16 years and 259 days old and would go on to make a further 134 League appearances for The Quakers in Division Four. He remembers fondly the antics of trainer Dickie Deacon who was one of football's famed characters. On one occasion a striker who had been dropped and scored a couple of goals for the reserves complained to Dickie demanding to know why he was in the second team - "...because we haven't got a third team" was the reply.

In the early days under Ray Yeoman, the promising young defender was recognised with a call-up to the England youth squad with, amongst others, Steve Perryman and Peter Taylor. He was selected for the final, reduced squad of sixteen and was sure that an international appearance would follow. However, manager Yeoman recalled him to play in the FA Cup against Scunthorpe refusing to release him to represent his country. This was a prime example of how clubs took advantage of - even exploited - players in the past. Nowadays, he believes it has swung too much the other way with players exploiting clubs and salaries spiraling out of control. Though he admits he would have liked to have been around when there was a little more cash in the game. His original weekly Feethams wage was £7 in the season and £5 in the summer rising to £50 when he moved up a notch to Carlisle United.

In 1972, the association with Darlington came to an acrimonious end when he took the club to a tribunal for the right to a free transfer - one of the first such cases. It was half way through a season that would see Darlington finish bottom of the Football League. His move to Carlisle in the Second Division saw him become a central figure in one of football's more romantic stories and The Cumbrians' most famous exploit. After promotion in 1973/74 behind Middlesbrough and Luton, Carlisle famously raced to the top of the First Division with successive victories over Liverpool and Chelsea. It was the dream of every small town club but sadly, short-lived. The team was picked from a tiny squad of seventeen players but unfortunately they simply couldn't score goals and eventually slipped to immediate relegation. The fairy tale was over.

Peter Carr can't believe his luck after having his wages doubled in a move to Carlisle in 1972 (Photo: Hartlepool Mail)

The legendary Chris Balderstone and the immovable Alan Ross in goal were the big names in the side and John Gorman - the one who became Glen Hoddle's right-hand man - was Peter's room-mate. Gorman was, and remains, a real gentleman whom Peter doubted was ruthless enough to make it in management. Interestingly, he has proved to be most successful as a number two. Peter loved his time at Brunton Park, missing only three games in the First Division and counting the promotion and subsequent adventure as one of his two most memorable times in football. The other was his move to America and the North American Soccer League.

Soccer in America was enjoying its first surge of popularity, with many of the game's greatest names competing in the fledgling league. His offer to cross the Atlantic consisted of doubling his wages at Carlisle and supplying him with a home and a car - mmm, let me think that one over. He decided to try it and played for the New England Teamen under Dennis Viollet and Noel Cantwell and the Washington Diplomats, for whom he operated as sweeper. Now, just read this list of names - Cruyff, Giles, Lorimer, Neeskens, Beckanbauar, Best, Carlos Alberto, Marsh, Brady, Hudson. Not to mention Mike Flanaghan, Roger Givens, Gerry Daly, Kevin Keelan and Keith Weller. These were the men he played with or against. Sweeping behind Cruyff in midfield was perhaps his greatest thrill, watching him do things with a ball that no other player was doing at the time. Crowds of sixty, seventy and eighty thousand were not uncommon and he remembers that you had to be good enough to play your own game and know your own space without assistance from team-mates, since you couldn't hear their voices because of the noise of the crowd. If you didn't have good positional sense, you didn't survive. He claims that Peter Simpson was so hard he used to eat hedgehog soup - with the spines on - and Gerry Daly was paid so much he took a wheelbarrow in on pay day. They were great days and are great memories.

In 1979 he returned home to play for Hartlepool in the American close season but was soon back in The States for good. After four more seasons, he quit aged thirty-two and made his home on the coast of New England. Now, he's not involved in the game. He watches occasionally, though not avidly and still keeps an eye on Darlington results. He was a player rather than a watcher and misses the camaraderie and the goose-bumps of those big matches. His mother and two sisters still give him reason to visit the North-East and, ever patriotic, he insists he will be buried in England - when the time comes, of course.

	Seasons	Apps	Goals	Source
Kenneth Chaytor (IF) Trimdon, 18 November 1937 Oldham Athletic	1954-59	77	20	JNRS

Interviewed September 2002

Known as 'The Durham Wonder Boy', Kenny Chaytor was snatched from the eager grasp of Sunderland by the charm of the Oldham player-manager, ex England and Great Britain captain, George Hardwick. The Roker Park manager, Bill Murray had been so keen to sign him that arrangements had already been made for young Kenny to start work as an apprentice electrician at Hartlepool while playing as a youth at Sunderland. However, in April 1953, aged 15 1/2, the young Chaytor was picked up from Trimdon in person by Hardwick and taken to his new lodgings in Oldham. It was the day before the final match of the season versus Bradford City that would see The Latics promoted to Division Two. The club was an attractive proposition and the chance of a quick rise to the first-team was the main reason, other than the charisma of Hardwick, that Kenny chose East Lancs over Wearside. He had been introduced to the club by trainer, Owen Willoughby, as a thirteen-year-old so also felt a sense of loyalty to the club. An apprentice

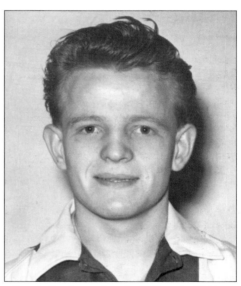

Dennis Bergkamp signs for Oldham in 1954– or is it Kenny Chaytor?

toolmaker's job at Wildings was arranged for the youngster who shone in the 'A' team, scoring a bagful of goals as the first eleven endured a rough ride in the higher Division followed by immediate relegation back to the Third Division (North).

Kenny was homesick but training two nights a week, going to night school, writing home and going to the pictures kept him busy. And while landlady, Mrs Holt was force-feeding him rice pudding and cheese 'n' onion sandwiches (he had once said that he liked them), the football was going from strength to strength. The ex Durham County schoolboy (where his team-mate was fellow Trimdoner, Bobby Laverick) enjoyed a meteoric rise from school football in the Kelloe League, to the 'A' team at Oldham, to his League debut within eighteen months. It was a 2-2 draw at Gateshead that provided Kenny with his first taste of the realities of the professional game at the tender age of 16 years and 339 days. Infamous Redheugh Park wing-half Tom Callender welcomed the debutant with the words "come near me and I'll break your bloody legs." The big defender shook his hand and said 'well done' at the final whistle but Kenny was so exhausted and excited after the game that he collapsed at the bus stop after being dropped off at Ferryhill with his mother and father. The club sent him for extensive tests but doctors put it down to the occasion.

Undeterred, he went on to score a League hat-trick at the age of 17 yrs and 2 months in a 3-1 victory over Mansfield giving credibility to Hardwick's youth policy. He didn't get to keep the match ball because the club didn't have enough to spare and he was denied a fourth goal when after being brought down by the 'keeper he was told he was 'too inexperienced' to take penalties. The spot kick was duly missed. However, Kenny's performances were now attracting the attentions of First Division clubs Manchester City and Sheffield United. It is alleged that Sheffield offered Oldham a record fee for a teenager to take him to Bramhall Lane. Oldham wouldn't do the deal and he only found out years later. Perhaps it was the words of George Hardwick that prevented them from cashing in their chips at that time. After signing Kenny as a part-time professional (wages the princely sum of £6 in winter and £4 in summer) on his seventeenth birthday the player-manager said, "With luck, he'll play for England before he's twenty. He's the only boy I've had who didn't need to be taught anything."

It was a great time to play in the north-west of England with Lancashire Cup and Combination matches pitting him against the likes of Charlton, Pegg, Byrne, Coleman - "a brilliant player," - Whelan and Taylor from Manchester Utd. However, the greatest he encountered was Duncan Edwards - a colossus. "One minute he was defending; the next he was scoring a goal. They hammered us out of sight. Twice." Nights out at the Savoy or Hills Store dance, where he met future wife June and the chance to go to Maine Road and Old Trafford on your days off added to the excitement of those early years. These were good times. Kenny was an England youth trialist and hot football property.

Unfortunately, when Hardwick left the club in 1956, so did Kenny's hopes of prolonged success at Boundary Park. He didn't like the new manager Ted Goodier, a man not given to the subtleties of the beautiful game. A man who at the beginning of the season when the players were given their chitty to buy new boots in town, advised that they should go for the old Hotspurs with high ankles and hard toe-caps because they were "good for clogging with". This summed up the problem with the relationship and as Kenny got fewer first-team chances his confidence began to ebb. By the time he had signed as a full-time pro' (wages £13 a-week) with the new manager, Norman Dodgin in 1958, his form had followed his confidence and he was eventually released in 1960. One incident in those later years demonstrated just how much the game has changed since then. Billy Spurdle had joined the club from Manchester City and was soon organising the benefit game his time at Maine Road had entitled him to. He tried to attract Stanley Matthews whose notorious demands were too high but was grateful for the appearance of Len Shackleton whose only request was for a Cup Final ticket. Most of the final tickets had gone to the directors as usual but one was raffled amongst the players. Kenny won the ticket but was happy to sell it for £2 to Spurdle who then gave it to Shackleton as an appearance fee. No such thing as player power in 1958.

There followed three happy and successful seasons with Witton Albion in the Cheshire League and Ashton Utd in the Lancashire Combination where the football was enjoyable again, the crowds decent and the money good. Then in 1964 he returned with wife and children, to the North-East. A trial for Darlington resulted in an injured toe and although he was asked back, the injury persisted and he eventually gave up hope of returning to the professional game. After a brief lay-off he resumed playing in the local leagues.

There were plenty of highlights in the Chaytor career - the League debut, the Mansfield hat-trick, the England trial, playing alongside the great George Hardwick and against the legendary Busby Babes. The lowest point was not being retained by Oldham in 1960. On reflection, he thinks that maybe he should have signed full-time at seventeen. Perhaps that would have given him a greater push into the game. However, if you ask whether or not he would repeat his ten years as a professional footballer, the answer is an unequivocal yes - "It was a great experience." These days, the man once known as 'the new Wilf Mannion' is an armchair Boro fan and sports fanatic. He's now retired in Trimdon with his wife, June (hello mother) and two artificial hips.

	Seasons	Apps	Goals	Source
Bryan Conlon (CF)				
Shildon, 14 January 1943, Died October 2000				
Newcastle Utd	1961	0	0	JNRS
Darlington	1964-67	74	27	South Shields
Millwall	1967-68	41	13	TR
Norwich City	1968-69	29	8	TR
Blackburn Rovers	1970-71	45	7	TR
Crewe Alexander	1971	4	1	L
Cambridge Utd	1971-72	18	3	TR
Hartlepool Utd	1972-73	41	3	TR

Despite a career that took him the length and breadth of the country, Bryan Conlon was Shildon through and through. He was born and raised there, married a Shildon girl in the parish church, played for the town team in 1974-75 when amateur status had been abolished. He finally died there after a long illness on 11th October 2000.

He was taken to Newcastle as a junior in 1961 but never made the first team. However, at the age of twenty-one his League career began in earnest when Jack Watson, the Darlington chief scout, lured him to Feethams from South Shields. He was the classic 'big centre-forward', a target man and a tireless worker for the team who helped the club to promotion from the Fourth Division in 1965-66 only to see them relegated the following season. His form was good enough to see him elevated to the Second Division with Millwall in 1967 where he played under Benny Fenton for two years before moving on to Carrow Road, Norwich in the same Division under the stewardship of his former Darlington manager Lol Morgan.

Another move within the Second Division took him to Ewood Park, Blackburn under John Carey where he suffered the disappointment of relegation to the Third Division in 1970-71. The next season saw him struggling to make the first eleven and a loan period at Crewe Alexander preceded a permanent move to Cambridge United of the Fourth Division. Eventually, the wanderer returned to his native north-east with a move to Len Ashurst's Hartlepool where, at thirty-one, his days as a League performer came to an end. After 252 games, 62 goals and 8 League clubs, he returned from whence he came - Shildon.

	Seasons	Apps	Goals	Source
Colin Cooper (D)				
Sedgefield, 28 February 1967	Eu21-8, E-2			
Middlesbrough	1985-90	188	6	JNRS
Millwall	1991-92	77	6	TR
Nottingham Forest	1993-98	180	20	TR
Middlesbrough	1998-2000	85	3	TR

Interviewed January 2002

Colin Cooper emerged as the most successful of a group of boys who were born in Trimdon in the late sixties and all went on to be signed by League clubs. Contemporaries Andrew Strong, Michael Trotter, David Young and John Tinkler all played in the Football League after turning out for the same school and youth club teams whilst growing up. Arguably, others had more natural ability but Colin's determination and resolve ensured that he capitalised on the opportunity he was given at Middlesbrough, where he made his League debut as an eighteen-year-old in a 0-2 defeat to Hull City at Ayresome Park in the 1985-86 relegation season. Sinking into the old Third Division

Colin Cooper scores for Middlesbrough versus Luton Town in 1988 – even he can't remember this one
(Photo: Paul Thompson)

would coincide with the club's near demise as it went into liquidation only to re-emerge the next season as a re-formed company with support from Middlesbrough Council. This re-birth was described by Colin as 'a great adventure' and a 'magical time' as the young team under the guidance of Bruce Rioch rose to the First Division and fell back to the Second by 1989.

Rioch's departure in1990 was followed by a bad injury to Colin in what proved to be his final year at Ayresome Park. Now managing Second Division Millwall, the former Boro boss parted with £300,000 to take his trusted charge to The Den where Colin consolidated his position as one of the country's most promising defenders, ultimately under new manager, Mick McCarthy

However, it was at Nottingham Forest where Colin ascended to his professional summit. Promotion from the First Division to the Premiership in 1993-94, his first season by the Trent, was followed by third place in The Premiership and the quarter-finals of the UEFA Cup against Bayern Munich in 1996. But his proudest footballing achievement came with his two Full England caps in the Umbro Cup in 1995. A 1-3 defeat to Brazil and a spectacular 3-3 draw with Sweden were career highlights. He will be forever grateful to Terry Venables though he was slightly disappointed not to retain his place in the subsequent national squad. It was also at Forest where he believes he became a more sophisticated player after the new guidelines on tackling from behind. In a newspaper interview he said he "had to become less impetuous....I'm sure I have become a bit more clever and as a result it has helped me be a better player." Frank Clarke was the man who had transformed Colin into a Premiership and international performer after spending £1,700,000 to take him to the City Ground. Stan Collymore was to be his next signing as the team was re-built following the sad end to the Cloughie years. Colin had a great deal of respect for Clarke and for the erratic Stan who was 'one of the lads' one minute and 'blowing up' the next but always 'scored for fun'.

Relegation followed by immediate promotion back to the Premiership under Dave Bassett marked the end of Colin's Nottingham adventure before Bryan Robson lured him back home to Middlesbrough, re-born in the magnificent Riverside Stadium. Colin regarded Robson's interest as a great compliment and the £2.5 million price tag took his total transfer fees to £4.5 million, the highest of all of the Sedgefield pro's. The move teamed him with the likes of Paul Gascoigne, Hamilton Ricard and Gary Pallister, confirming his status as one of the top professionals in the country.

However, now thirty-five, Colin is aware that he is nearing the end of a distinguished playing career. He's proud to have counted Pallister, Mowbray, Collymore, Pearce, Gazza, Ince and Shearer as colleagues and has a special word for managers Clarke, Robson, Rioch and Maddren. Currently in and out of the team under Steve McClaren, he is at the stage where the future is a real consideration. His contract takes him to the end of the 2003/04 season and he is determined to play on as long as possible, happy to drop out of the Premiership if necessary to continue a career with his boots on. But after it's over - management? Coaching? Media work? He's not sure. Seventeen successful years in the game have allowed him to provide for his wife and children in a way he could only have dreamt of as a boy. So, as he sees it, "I've had one good life - now it's time to consider the next one."

	Seasons	Apps	Goals	Source
Gordon Cowans (M)				
Cornforth, 27 October 1958 Eyth/Eu21-5/E'B'/E-10				
Aston Villa	1975-84	286	42	APP
Aston Villa	1988-91	117	7	Bari (It)
Blackburn Rovers	1991-92	50	2	TR
Aston Villa	1993	11	0	TR
Derby County	1993-94	36	0	TR
Wolverhampton Wanderers	1994-95	37	0	TR
Sheffield Utd	1995	20	0	TR
Bradford City	1996	24	0	TR
Stockport County	1996	7	0	TR
Burnley (N/C)	1997	6	0	TR

Gordon Cowans was a gifted midfielder recognised at the highest level with ten full international caps for his country and although he played professionally for nine clubs, he will forever be associated with Aston Villa. He played at Villa Park for thirteen of his twenty-two seasons as a League performer and during the first spell was a member of the team that won the League Cup, League Championship, European Cup and Super Cup under Ron Saunders.

A County Durham and District Schoolboy representative, he was signed as an apprentice by Aston Villa in 1974, turning professional in August 1976. By this time he had already made his League debut against Manchester City at Maine Road as a seventeen-year-old and by the end of the season, he was an established Villan. The honours came thick and fast. He had represented England Youth in the 1976 Monaco Tournament and was drafted to the under-21 team. The League Cup Final win over Everton in 1977 was followed by the Young Player of the Year award in1979/80 and the magical purple patch in 1980/81 when Villa could claim to be the best in Europe. A call-up to the England B team was followed closely by promotion to the full international team in 1983 against Wales at Wembley, the first of his ten full caps.

Europe and Serie 'A' beckoned when Bari signed him in 1985 and he became one of England's more successful exports, playing out four seasons with the Italians before returning for his second spell with Villa and gaining the last of his international caps versus the Republic of Ireland. His career took him on a long and winding journey covering the North and Midlands for the next seven years finishing at Second Division Burnley at the age of thirty-nine. There was only one place to go after that - and so it was that Gordon Cowans returned to Aston Villa as a coach. He is still there and is revered to the extent that he is one of twenty-nine 'Club Legends' listed on the Aston Villa web-site. He did quite well really.

	Seasons	Apps	Goals	Source
Robert Cowell (FB)				
Trimdon, 5 December 1922 Died 1996				
Newcastle Utd	1946-54	289	0	Blackhall Colliery

Bobby Cowell's place in Newcastle United's history will be for ever secure as one of only three players to have appeared in all three FA Cup winning teams from the 1950's. He was in exalted company, the other two being Bobby Mitchell and Jackie Milburn. One of his most memorable moments was a headed goal-line clearance in the 1951 final when Stan Mortenson of Blackpool nodded the ball beyond the United 'keeper, Fairbrother. The score was 0-0 at the time and the dramatic save turned the game, which Newcastle eventually won 2-0. Bobby reckoned he made about £22 from those three final appearances but he wasn't one to begrudge the modern players their huge salaries. His only regret was not being offered complimentary tickets to watch his successors in black and white attempting to emulate the great team of the '50's. Incidentally, his debut was against Newport County in 1946. United won 13-0 and a certain Len Shackleton, recently signed from Bradford Park Avenue, scored a double hat-trick. Bobby made 408 appearances in all competitions having started as a wartime player, spotted playing for Blackhall Colliery. His beginnings had been as son of a Trimdon Grange mining family and he had originally turned out in the local leagues where his own childhood heroes played. But his was destined to be a career played out at the highest level with some of the greatest footballers of his generation in a team hailed as probably the greatest in the history of Newcastle United.

Regrettably, at the age of thirty-three and playing in a European friendly match in 1955, Bobby sustained an injury, which forced him to retire from the game. It meant that his final appearance in the Newcastle first team in England was in fact the 1955 FA Cup Final victory over Manchester City. His contribution to the Newcastle legend was rewarded with a testimonial game attended by 36,000 fans. It was the first post-war testimonial for a Magpies' player. Bobby Cowell eventually retired to live in his adopted Ponteland and was an avid black and white fan to the end, which came following a stroke in 1996. He remains a Newcastle United legend.

Sir Bobby Robson, the current Magpies manager recently disclosed at a dinner in his honour that Bobby was one of his great heroes and an inspiration for his own career. There can't be too many better accolades than that.

	Seasons	Apps	Goals	Source
Stanley Cummins (M)				
Ferryhill, 6 December 1958				
Middlesbrough	1976-79	44	9	APP
Sunderland	1979-82	133	29	TR
Crystal Palace	1983-84	28	7	TR
Sunderland	1984	17	0	TR

Interviewed July 1999

Stan Cummins became famous as the player Jack Charlton allegedly claimed would be the first million pound footballer. In fact, what he did say was that it wouldn't be long before a young player was sold for £1 million and that Stan was in that category. But the misquote became a truth and Stan had to bear this epithet for the rest of his career. He had debuted against Ipswich Town at the age of 17 after being with Middlesbrough since 14 and had the pleasure of playing alongside Graham Souness, whom he regards as one of the great modern footballers, and England fullback, Terry Cooper. His days at Ayresome Park ended in 1979 when John Neal sold him to Sunderland for £300,000. But success was immediate as Ken Knighton's team achieved the runners-up position in the Second Division and was promoted to the top League behind Leicester City. The promotion game versus West Ham was one of the highlights of Stan's career.

His time at Sunderland was perhaps his most fulfilling, playing for the team he had supported as a boy and including moments like scoring on his debut and netting four against Burnley in May 1980. Three seasons in the First Division saw him tested at the highest level of the domestic game but he fell out of favour with new manager Alan Durban in 1984 and was sold on to Crystal Palace in the Second Division. This turned into the greatest regret of his career, rejecting an offer to move to Newcastle United where Arthur Cox had signed Kevin Keegan, in favour of The Eagles. On failing to sign Stan, Cox turned to Peter Beardsley and the rest is history. London didn't agree with him or his family and he returned to Sunderland later in 1984 under Len Ashurst. Unfortunately, he had to sit out the League Cup final defeat by Norwich City that season because he was cup-tied. He had appeared in an earlier round for Palace against Sunderland but having missed two great chances was blamed by the fans for the defeat.

Stan Cummins spent fifteen years in America losing his hair so that when he returned to England he would look like a manager – mission accomplished (Photo: Paul Thompson)

At the end of the season, Ashurst's brief tenure was ended by the fanfare arrival of Lawrie MacMenemy who was given unprecedented power at the club and went on to achieve an unprecedented level of failure, taking Sunderland into the Third Division. Stan also left, this time for the Minnesota Kicks in the NASL and Minnesota Strikers in the fledgling Major Indoor Soccer League where he starred in 6-a-side matches of one hours duration with four quarters of 15 minutes. In many ways America provided some of the most memorable moments in his career. Imagine playing against Pele, Beckenbaur and George Best who were drawing the crowds for the New York Cosmos. In fact, Stan Cummins is one person with a George Best anecdote, which involves a quiet night out in a peanut bar. The assembled company had a couple of civilised drinks, ate nuts and engaged in friendly, polite chat. The great man was apparently charming and sober - well at least not drunk.

One of the greatest memories for Stan was playing alongside Bobby Charlton in John Hickton's testimonial. Not only was this a special moment for an up and coming footballer but it reminded him of advice once offered by the scout, Ray Grant. He said there were two routes a talented footballer could take, the Best way with women and drink or the Charlton way, sensible and disciplined. Stan Cummins chose the Charlton way, married early and spent wisely.

And so Stan Cummins' football career ended amongst the glitz of soccer USA style. He remained in America, where he took dual nationality, but not in football. He lived and worked in Kansas with his wife and three children, employed by a carpet company and an avid fan of the English Premiership which he watched every Sunday at home. He always looked out for results at Sunderland, Middlesbrough and Hartlepool where his friend, Chris Turner is manager and occasionally gets the urge to play again. So far, he's resisted the urge but would relish the opportunity to make it in coaching or management , so much so that he has recently returned to England to rekindle his career in football. But deep down, he knows he'll always be remembered by football fans as the diminutive but dynamic talent who might have cost a million pounds.

	Seasons	Apps	Goals	Source
William Curley (FB)				
Trimdon, 20 Nov 1945				
Darlington	1962-64	29	1	APP

Interviewed March 2000

Bill Curley's claim to fame is that he was the first ever apprentice professional at Darlington, signed as a sixteen year old in 1962 by Eddie Carr. His debut was at Sinsil Bank against Lincoln City after travelling down on the coach as the twelfth man. Regular full-back, Bobby Whitehead was carrying an injury and not sure to play. However, it was only twenty minutes before kick-off when Bill got the call. He was given a torrid time by the Lincoln winger in the first half but some friendly advice from the sidelined Whitehead at the interval enabled him to play the winger out of the game in the second period. His next opportunity was away to League newcomers Oxford United. However, this time it was Bill carrying an injury and unable to take the field. From then on he was in and out of the team and struggling to break into his favourite left-back position, which was by now occupied by player-manager, Lol Morgan.

Bill was a contemporary of other local lads, Mike Peacock, John Hope, John Heaviside who twice replaced him at left-back, Brian Conlon and Malcolm Dawes. Bill recalls that he used to travel to reserve matches courtesy of Macolm's old green van as the two of them took their first steps on the professional ladder. His chief memory of Brian Conlon was the celebration and civic reception that followed Dalington's promotion in 1965-66. Bill 'got blotto' and crashed out at Brian's place - the only way to celebrate.

Bill's closest sniff of the big time came in the 1964-65 season when, after beating local rivals Hartlepool 4-1 in an FA Cup 2nd round replay, they were drawn at home to Arsenal. Manager Lol Morgan decided to play himself so consigning Bill to twelfth man. He still remembers sitting in the dressing room as the Arsenal team filed past the open door - Frank Mclintock, George Armstrong, Joe Baker and manager, Billy Wright. He recalls with commendable honesty that he hoped Lol Morgan had a 'stinker'. He did and was roundly booed by the home crowd.

It was another full-back, John Peverell, who eventually claimed the regular spot in the team prompting a transfer request from Bill in November 1965. He continued to play in the reserves but unfortunately injured his cruciate ligament in a game at Roker Park against a Sunderland second eleven boasting youngsters John O'Hare and Colin Todd. The injury restricted him to two more reserve team outings before he was placed on the FIFA list and eventually contacted by a team from Adelaide. Bill had played his last League game and emigrated to Australia on an assisted passage scheme in January 1967, only weeks after getting married. He played full-time for the USC Lions (what else but the Ukranian Sports Club). It was a useful standard, not unlike Conference football today. However, the cruciate didn't stand the pace and Bill finally called it a day at the age of twenty-two. He joined the New South Wales prison service to begin a career that would take him through to retirement. Returning to England in October 1969 he joined the British service and finally settled in the Leeds area, feeding prisoners at Armley and bringing up three children as good Yorkshire folk.

His brightest memories are of his League debut and of the only goal he scored, an eighteen yard thumper that cannoned in off the goalkeeper's chest making Bill a hero for the day with the Darlington supporters. His most revered playing colleague was Howard Kendal with whom he lined up for Durham County Boys v Lancashire Boys at Feethams. This was only a year or so before Kendal became the youngest cup finalist with Preston North End. The opponent he most admired was Bobby Smith of Brighton, the former Tottenham and England centre-forward whom Bill remembers as 'a big dirty bugger with massive thighs'. Now that's what I call an epitaph.

 **is for Commentary**

Clubs, pubs and other people's houses. These are the places I watch live football on Sky television. I loathe and despise everything Rupert Murdoch stands for and steadfastly refuse to buy into any aspect of his media empire. Anyway, why should the great British sporting occasions be denied to those who don't own a dish? This way I delude myself that I am actually ripping him off. The other advantage is experiencing that semi-live atmosphere of a room full of blokes full of beer who are substituting the terrace for the taproom. This enables one to benefit from the wisdom of comments both on the screen and in the bar.

So let me take you back to the occasion of January 18th 1995 when I was in attendance at the club to watch the Newcastle Utd versus Blackburn Rovers FA Cup third round tie at Ewood Park. — "The ground that Jack built", as Steve Sutton so imaginatively put it on Look North. The first cliché of the night. Further expert opinion was soon forthcoming during the game:

"That Flowers is a bloody good keeper. Class!!" - Proceeds to be beaten by a banana shot from Marc Hottiger, a Swiss fullback who has never before scored for Newcastle and a near post hoof from Lee Clarke.

"Don't rate Peacock at all. Ordinary." - Proceeds to dominate in defence a la Bobby Moore.

"Shearer's got to be the best since Lofthouse." - Proceeds to play like a complete fart. Couldn't score in a brothel you might say.

To add to the entertainment, Martyn Tyler delivers one of the most tortured and contrived one liners ever to emanate from the cliché factory - "This match has all the classic cut and traditional thrust of the FA Cup." What a load of alliterative bollocks.

It is, of course, discussion, comment and opinion that fuels the passions within the game of football. Everyone is an expert and everyone wrong. It's a pity that some TV commentators try too hard to wrap up their comments in neat little phrases that have become known as 'sound bites'. Too often it just doesn't work. However, when it does they rank alongside quotations by Wilde or Churchill and can rival the poetry of Shakespeare.

My absolute favourite comes not from football but from an Olympic hockey match between Great Britain and Germany. The British have just scored a vital goal and Barry Davies simply cannot contain himself having seen the German defence split asunder.

" You have to ask where were the Germans? But frankly, who cares."

Now that's what I call objectivity.

The 'D' Team

	Seasons	Apps	Goals	Source
Aiden Davison (G)				
Sedgefield, 11 May 1968 NIB-1, NI-3				
Notts County	1988	1	0	Billingham Synthonia
Bury	1989	0	0	TR
Millwall	1991-92	34	0	TR
Bolton Wanderers	1993-95	37	0	TR
Hull City	1996	9	0	L
Bradford City	1996	10	0	TR
Grimsby Town	1997-99	77	0	TR
Sheffield United	1999	2	0	TR
Bradford City	1999-2000	8	0	L/TR

Interviewed June 2001

A cursory glance at the playing statistics of Aiden Davison would suggest that you are looking at the classic career profile of a journeyman footballer. However, perhaps the phrase, 'have gloves will travel' would be more appropriate. Currently at Bradford City, Aiden has played at nine League clubs not counting a number of others to whom he has been loaned. The term journeyman also suggests someone who has plugged away gamely at his career but achieved little of note. However, if you dig deeper you find a player who has appeared three times at full international level for Northern Ireland, has spent three seasons in the Premier League and won the Auto Windscreen Trophy and promotion to the First Division with Grimsby. In addition he was player of the year at First Division Millwall, kept a club record 35 clean sheets for Grimsby and was on the Bolton bench for the League Cup Final defeat by Liverpool in 1995. On closer inspection, this is a career of some achievement.

Born in Sedgefield but brought up around Bishop Auckland, he was a non-league performer at Spennymoor and Bishop Auckland whilst working at the Eldon brickworks. He'd been watched by a number of clubs but was eventually lured to Notts County by John Barnwell who had returned to the game after a serious car crash and was 'a pleasure to work with'. Garys Birtles and Mills, Tommy Johnstone and David Rush were amongst his team-mates but things didn't work out after Barnwell left and Neil Warnock took over. His one appearance and League debut came in a 0-3 defeat at Preston on the infamous astroturf then he was sold on to Bury under Sam Ellis. Unfortunately this was an unhappy time professionally and Aiden felt he learned a lot of the negative aspects of the game during this period. Gary Kelly was first choice in goal and Aiden was forced to take loan spells at Chester and Blackpool.

The real breakthrough came on his transfer to Millwall in 1991 when Bruce Rioch recognised his potential and two successful seasons followed. It was here he developed a friendship with Colin Cooper and had a run to the FA Cup 5th round with 'The Lions'. However, when Rioch left for Bolton, his chances of continued success at Millwall receded. But when one door closes, another opens. Rioch moved for his old 'keeper and Aiden transferred to Bolton for £25,000. There followed three seasons of success for the club with promotion, a year in The Premiership and a League Cup final appearance, though for the most part Aiden played second fiddle to Keith Branaghan. However, it was a sweet taste of the Premiership champagne existence and a chance to mix it with the new foreign stars he believes have added so much excitement to the game in England.

'The Three Amigoalies' – Matt Clarke, Gary Walsh and Aiden Davison – all of Bradford City FC

When Rioch left again he was loaned out to Hull City in the Third Division. This completed his journey through every division of The League and put him in the shop window for a move to Bradford which, initially based on a loan deal, became permanent when the Yorkshire club were obliged to take on his old Bolton contract. This brief spell at Valley Parade was followed by something more permanent at Blundell Park, Grimsby where he enjoyed consistent first team football and a growing reputation. However, the nomad instinct kicked in again at the end of his contract and he took advantage of the Bosman ruling to move across Yorkshire to Sheffield United and Adrian Heath. Not a good decision. After two games, a trial and injury at Chelsea, the resignation of Heath and the arrival of the inevitable Warnock, he was off again. However, on this occasion the loan spell back at Bradford turned out to be an inspired choice. Two seasons with a Premiership club, one of which saw The Bantams survive a thrilling, nerve jangling relegation dog-fight, represented another taste of the big time. Even though he has had to settle for reserve status to Matt Clarke and Gary Walsh, Aiden has retained his position at the club and continued to serve them well when called upon. He wonders what will happen to Bradford though. He claims it's what the professionals call 'a pub team'. It has a poor infrastructure, an ineffective youth policy, little cash for transfers and a chairman, Geoffrey Richmond, whom some believe gave manager, Jim Jeffries, only half-hearted support. There have been some great players at the club - Benny Carbone, the best he's appeared with, is a marvellous talent but not the grafter that the club needed.

International caps in 1996, 97 and 98 are his proudest moments, his debut coming in a 0-1 defeat by Sweden at Windsor Park and his last coming in a 1-3 defeat at the hands of Germany, Oliver Bierhoff the late executioner. He sat on the bench for over twenty more and feels unfortunate not to have gained more caps. He also feels honoured to have worked with Peter Shilton, his goalkeeping hero and other greats, Pat Jennings and Ray Clemence. Oh, and when asked who should be the current England number one he is quite emphatic - David James.

He takes a very pragmatic view of his career now. It's a great profession but it is also his living. Getting a contract is all-important and he is already planning for the day when the Football League passes him by for a younger pair of gloves. He'll probably go to the United States with his American wife and children. Until then he wants to play as long as possible. After all, it's what he does.

	Seasons	Apps	Goals	Source
Malcolm Dawes (D)				
Trimdon, 3 March 1944				
Darlington	1962	0	0	
Aldershot	1965-69	163	2	Horden Colliery
Hartlepool Utd	1970-75	195	12	TR
Workington	1975-76	51	1	TR

Interviewed June 2002

There aren't too many players in world football who can claim to have been replaced by Pele but Malcolm Dawes is one of them. Alright, it's stretching a point really but it is a fact that as Malcolm was placed on the transfer list by New York Cosmos before the 1975 American soccer season, Pele was signed up to add some selling power to the team. Malcolm had completed two summers in the USA and would compete in one more for Denver Colorados before bringing to an end a three-year marathon, non-stop footballing adventure.

However, this was all a far cry from the Plantation estate in Trimdon Grange where the Dawes family resisted the bulldozers and remained in one of the last two houses to stand before clearance was complete. He'd been football mad, kicking around balls of old rags and a pigs bladder before graduating to a real ball, which he painted white to keep up with the times. His heroes were the local talent, particularly Jimmy Cain,

Malcolm Dawes receives his Hartlepool player of the year award in 1974 and simultaneously auditions for a part in Starsky and Hutch

who would often turn up at Northside field just along from the family home. Stanley Matthews was the 'famous' hero and it was the Stan Matthews boots that were the first to adorn the Dawes feet - nailed in studs and all. But it was soon Malcolm who was catching the eye and Darlington was first out of the blocks to sign him. Manager Eddie Carr made him a professional on his eighteenth birthday in 1962 but after a year on the side-lines he was released and moved south to Nuneaton in the Southern League for £10 a-week and £5 appearance money. The closest he had come to a League debut whilst at Feethams was when he travelled as twelfth man to Crewe. George Luke had been ill and it looked certain that Malcolm would start. Unfortunately, Luke was risked and was so ill he collapsed at half-time only to be revived, slapped around a bit and sent back on. With no substitutes, Malcolm missed out on his long awaited first taste of The Football League.

He was impressed by the Southern League but failed to agree further terms and returned north to Horden where he teamed up with old hero, Jimmy Cain. However, in 1965, whilst visiting his soldier brother in Aldershot and taking a pint in the supporters club, he was approached by manager Dave Smith to come for a trial. The deal was done and for four full seasons after his break through, Malcolm enjoyed a consistent run of appearances and form in a team perpetually just short of promotion. He enjoyed his time at the Recreation Ground but was on his way out as soon as Jimmy Melia arrived. Melia had been a top class player with Liverpool, Wolves, Southampton and England but had not found it easy to 'step down' to the lower leagues. After a disasterous own goal against Darlington, Melia set about Malcolm with a volley of scouse sarcasm that provoked a strong reaction. Malcolm 'went for' Melia - he played eight more games for The Shots and was transferred. Needless to say, Malcolm Dawes and Jimmy Melia did not get along. In Malcolm's own words - well actually, I can't use his words.

The following season Hartlepool and Rochdale competed for the Dawes signature and it was a good two-year deal and the promise of other useful signings that drew Malcolm back to the North-East. However, manager, John 'Whistler' Simpson - "a lovely bloke" - paid the price for a poor campaign and was replaced by Len Ashurst. The new manager was naïve but a good listener and learner. The players liked him and he survived for three moderate seasons, the highlight of which was the introduction of Tony Toms, an ex-commando fitness trainer. Training had never been so interesting - or so hard. Malcolm recalls track racing at Grayfields, where he managed to win a mile race against the likes of Willie Waddell, Bill Green and Neil Warnock in a respectable four and a half minutes. The same training methods were responsible for John Coyne filling his pants during a 100 metre dash.

Hartlepool was a happy, welcoming club and this was the happiest phase of Malcolm's career. His famed fitness allowed him to compete in the Fourth Division in the English season and in America during the summer. Ex Carlisle wing-half, Gordon Bradley was coaching in The States and was trying to sign players to help boost the fledgling American professional game. These were early days in the selling of soccer stateside but Malcolm learned more from the Americans about marketing and promotion than in a lifetime in England. The football was great fun, the social life even better. Warner Brothers owned the New York Cosmos, enabling the players to access all manner of top class entertainment and the pace was no less hectic in Denver. Elvis, Sinatra, Roberta Flack, Jose Feliciano and Sugar Ray Leonard were amongst those whom Malcolm would never have seen but for his time over the pond. Perhaps his biggest regret, however, was just missing out on meeting and playing with Pele. In a pre-season press-call to announce the great man's impending signing by The Cosmos a five-a-side exhibition was to be staged. Everything was set to go when suddenly Pele was withdrawn from the match by his people because of the crowds and the pressure. Still, as Pele anecdotes go, it's not bad.

Malcolm's two final League seasons were at Workington. He had injured his ankle at Hartlepool and lost his place in the team. Workington stepped in, he got a 'decent back-hander', signed a permanent deal and played against Bournemouth on the Saturday following his father's death on the Monday. If football is your job, you can't afford to hang around. In fact, in his final season he was offered the position of player-coach. It meant a different relationship with his team-mates and at a struggling club, a job description that included scouting, washing shirts, coaching - everything. Manager Alan Ashman couldn't halt the decline and was eventually replaced by Colin Meldrum who had already replaced Malcolm as coach. Workington Town's fall reached terminal velocity in May 1977 when they finished bottom of The Football League and were relegated. Malcolm had by then already been on 'the sick' for ten weeks following a knee injury. He played one last game at Hartlepool before his own League career ended after 409 appearances in the Fourth Division.

The cartlidge had received no specialist treatment at Workington and continued to be a problem. He endured one operation after the relegation season, got a free transfer and played some Sunday football. One appearance for Scarborough versus Wigan in November 1977, was enough to convince him that another operation was necessary and it duly followed. Local leagues were his recreation from then on and he has since remained self-employed selling cleaning materials, coaching cricket for Durham schools and working with Durham County Cricket Club. He does some scouting for Shrewsbury and is active in organising sportsman's dinners. Still living in Sedgefield and still pulling on the boots for the over 40's, Malcolm Dawes is not a man to let the grass grow under his feet.

is for 'Dun Cow'

The Dun Cow in Sedgefield is one of those pubs you might expect to see in any stereotypical village photographed by American tourists but usually imagined to be in The Cotswolds. White fronted, adorned with flowers, boasting low slung beams and guest ales with names like 'Sheep Dip' and 'Dogs Bollocks', this could be the place of John Major's dreams when he spoke of old ladies cycling to church and cricket on the village green. Indeed, Sedgefield was once a Conservative blip on an otherwise straight line Labour graph in the district. Now it is New Labour. Tony Blair even brought his mate Lionel Jospin here for a pint to give it a truly European Socialist dimension. Ironically, we were on holiday in France at the time and switched on the TV only to see Sedgefield and the Dun Cow on all the French news programmes. True to form, Tony and Lionel did what all politicians apart from Kenneth Clarke do and simply allowed the beer to brush their lips for the sake of the cameras. I have a theory that this is not just to avoid appearing squiffy in public but also to avoid getting wind. Have you ever heard a politician fart?

However, on the 26th December, while the old ladies are cycling to church and the cricketers are linseeding their willow in preparation for pre-season nets, the Dun Cow is pure football. The over 40's play the Young'ns in the annual Boxing Day challenge when the game is, of course, a pre-cursor to the afternoon session and merely an excuse to have a few beers. The light headed generosity of spirit and interminable reminiscing which pervade the hours between one and six hint at what life must be like in that parallel universe where people are permanently happy.

It was on Boxing Day in 1996 amid the usual communal rendering of popular tunes and the exchange of very old jokes that a man in his early fifties with no shirt on could be found with his nose to the floor halfway through a press-up competition with a rather attractive young Australian girl. The girl won a handsome victory. Though I think it is fair to say that the strength to weight ratio diminishes rapidly after a gallon of ale, almost as quickly as the bravado to common sense ratio rises. But who cares? It's Boxing Day.

The man in question was Malcolm Dawes who, amongst other teams, has turned out for Workington Town and New York Cosmos but still has the enthusiasm and fitness to mark the 26th of December by dusting down the old magic and showing the youngsters a few tricks. It was in fact Malcolm who informed me exactly a year earlier that Trimdon's Bobby Cowell had suffered a stroke and was seriously ill. The ex-Newcastle fullback died a few days later but took his rightful place as a topic of football conversation in the Dun Cow.

Not that the pub is only a haven for old footballers. On the contrary. I recently witnessed Dion Dublin and Gary Pallister enjoying Sunday lunch with their respective partners. I can report that they looked as fit as butchers' dogs, indulged in no horseplay whatsoever and left the premises totally sober. I don't know what the modern game is coming to.

The 'E' Team

	Seasons	Apps	Goals	Source
Kevin Elliott (F) Chilton, 5 September 1958 Hartlepool Utd	1975-76	27	1	APP

Interviewed Father August 1999

You will not find Kevin Elliott's number in the local telephone directory. He's another of the ex-League players from the Sedgefield District to have packed his boots and passport to make a career abroad, in his case Australia. He left for Oz in 1982 marrying on the Sunday and emigrating on the Monday. He starred in the Australian League with another local lad, Matty Pearson and went on to win many honours in the game 'down under', where he became something of a celebrity for his sporting achievements.

Kevin Elliott receives the Golden Boot for top scorer in the Australian League while a strange man proposes marriage

However, it was Hartlepool United who set him on his own personal road to success. A talented performer for Chilton Juniors, he was taken to The Victoria Ground by manager Ken Hale at the age of sixteen and played first team football at seventeen. They were difficult times for Hartlepool. Mind you, they usually are. A reasonably comfortable 14th place in his first season was followed by an eleventh application for re-election to The League at the end of 1976-77. Hartlepool would go on to make a record 14 applications for re-election, all successful.

The 1976-77 season was memorable for three historic events connected with 'Pools, two of which involved Kevin Elliott. In November, as winter began to suggest itself, the team was defeated 0-1 by Third Division Chester City in the FA Cup first round. It wasn't a bad performance but the young inside-forward was sent-off to become the third of three Hartlepool players to be dismissed in the FA Cup in consecutive seasons, thus setting an FA Cup record. In a fairly miserable season which also included the 'Victoria Ground Saga', a wrangle with the local council over the ownership of the ground, 'Pools played Workington on 19th February in what was to be their last appearance at Hartlepool in their last ever League season. They were replaced by Wimbledon in the re-election pantomime with ex-Pool midfielder, Malcolm Dawes appearing for the Reds and also playing out his last League season. The final little slice of history was made after the annual re-election triumph when the club changed its name from Hartlepool AFC to Hartlepool United.

As for Kevin, he was released by manager Billy Horner in the close season and a few short years later, headed for the other side of the world, sponsored by an Australian firm. He now lives in Perth, Western Australia where he is a representative for a cigarette company and also coaches football and basketball in his spare time. In many ways, he has had the career in Australia that was denied him in Britain.

	Seasons	Apps	Goals	Source
Nichol Evans (OR) Trimdon, 23 November 1925 New Brighton (Am)	1946	1	0	Heseldon

Nick Evans was a talented non-league performer who occasionally trained and played with the reserves at the Victoria Ground, Hartlepool, where his father, Nick Evans Snr. was reserve team coach. However, his only appearance in the Football League was one episode in a bizarre and historic match. On 15th March 1947 the New Brighton team assembled to board the team bus to Hartlepool only to find that three of their players had been delayed by atrocious weather conditions. Undaunted, the other players and management staff set off north, arriving only minutes before kick-off but determined to complete the fixture. Neil McBain, the New Brighton manager, desperate to find a deputy for his absent goalkeeper, decided to take the gloves himself thus making him, at 52 years and four months, the oldest player ever to appear in a League match. In order to complete his team he signed Nick Evans on the spot as an amateur. He'd come to watch the game but found himself taking part in an historic footballing occasion. As Fred Clymo, a friend and fellow spectator said: " One minute I'm talking to him in the stand and the next time I see him, the bugger's racing up the wing." For the record, Hartlepool won 3-0 and New Brighton got a standing ovation from the 5,844 fans.

is for Existentialist Goalkeepers

"All I know most surely about morality and the obligations of man, I owe to football."

These words are attributed to Albert Camus the French-Algerian Philosopher and writer who was no mean performer between the sticks when he wasn't scratching his chin. It is just the sort of thing you would expect a drinking partner of Jean Paul Sartre to come out with, turning football into a metaphor for life. But you have to admit, it's a quotation straight out of the top drawer, much like the famous turn and volley that won goal of the month for Justin Fashanu and convinced people he was a great player. Or the George Best lob over half the Tottenham team including the 'keeper, which merely confirmed that he was.

True team sports are a microcosm of life. The strong, the weak, the inter-dependence, the courage, the striving, the submission, the achievement, the failure, the elation, the dejection. The naturally gifted and the honest grafters working together to reach a common goal. It's about learning and understanding about yourself and others. It's about making the most of the hand you are dealt. All human character is on display in team sports and football is the purest and least contrived of them all.

But is it a coincidence that Camus was a goalkeeper? Existentialism stresses the importance of personal experience and responsibility for the individual in a seemingly meaningless universe. Have you noticed how goalkeepers get better as they get older and are still playing when those around them have moved on to manage pubs? Have you noticed how many goalkeepers adopt strange, idiosyncratic practices designed to help them focus on their singular task? Isn't it true that goalkeepers have a peculiarly individual role within a team game that is often played out in front of and around them? You don't have to be an existentialist to be a goalie but it helps — "I keep goal therefore I am."

All of the above would suggest that I concur with the view that goalkeepers are a race apart. Well I think they probably are. After all, it is widely believed that there is a certain madness which inhabits most 'keepers. And I have to say I recognize this trait in many of those I have played with and against. One of John Burridge's trainers said to him as a fifteen-year-old starting off in the game: "Son, goalkeepers have got to be crackers and daft. You son, have the qualities of an international." He took it as a compliment. Then there was Terry Yorath summing up Neville Southall in 1993: "I wouldn't go so far as to say he's a complete nutcase, but he comes very close to it."

However, it's Barry Davies who does it again for me with another classic piece of commentary from 1987 which proves beyond doubt that goalies are in fact aliens:

"Lukic saved with his foot which is all part of the goalkeepers arm."

Can there be any doubt?

The 'F' Team

	Seasons	Apps	Goals	Source
Thomas Flockett (FB)				
Ferryhill, 17 July 1927 Died 1997				
Chesterfield	1949-56	200	1	Spennymoor Utd
Bradford City	1957-62	227	1	TR

Interviewed Brother March 1999

Tom Flockett was another product of the North-Eastern League which offered the opportunity for payment as opposed to the 'strictly amateur' status of the Northern League. He was signed as a professional by Chesterfield from Spennymoor Utd having shown initial promise for Dean Bank Juniors. Playing in the Second Division of the Football League gave Tom the opportunity to match himself against opposition of genuine quality. In fact, it was up against the great Tom Finney in a game with Preston North End that Tom broke his leg in 1951. Preston went on to top the division and win promotion to the First with Manchester City, while Chesterfield finished second bottom and were relegated to the Third with Grimsby.

He continued as a regular at Saltergate until being transferred to Bradford City by Teddy Davison in 1957. Unfortunately he was to suffer another relegation when the Valley Parade team under Peter Jackson, slipped into the Fourth Division where Tom played out his final season. He worked in a glass factory after his football career had finished and remained in the Chesterfield area until his death in 1997.

is for Floodlights

There is something about football under floodlights that evokes an atmosphere which is quite different from daylight games. Evening dew sparkling on the grass, plumes of steam rising from panting players, the muffled sound of gloved hands beating together and the beckoning glow of the stadium set against a black night sky as you approach the ground. Think of British football and this is the image you will probably conjure up.

There are basically three types of floodlight in the professional game. There are those mounted in rows along the edges of stadium roofs. There are those arranged in a neat square at the top of pylons in the corner of the ground angling their beams so that each player has four shadows. Then, finally there are those at Brunton Park. As you approach Carlisle United's ground down the Warwick Road, you will see three pylons with lights arranged in a strange triangular fashion. The fourth corner has lights mounted on the roof of the new East stand. These pointy pylons have often, in my experience, been several bulbs short of a full quota giving the impression that Michael Knighton had found a new way of saving money.

Of course, the lights over Brunton could be those of an extra terrestrial craft hovering above the turf in readiness to re-claim the United 'keeper who is one of their own. He has been sent on a mission to earth, told to assume the appearance of an average human (a goalie is the nearest he can achieve) and report back on 'this activity they call football'. The alien beings are intrigued by these tribal gatherings which apparently affect the whole planet and for some unknown reason

they have made contact through Michael Knighton. Some have derided him as a crackpot for suggesting he had a close encounter not realising the future of our civilization is in his hands. Why do you think he resisted selling Tony Caig who was clearly a goalkeeper capable of playing in a higher division? Makes you think, doesn't it?

Many younger fans will take illumination for granted not realising that there were times when matches routinely kicked off before 3.00pm in order to finish in daylight. In fact, it was 22nd February 1956 before lights were used at a League match. The Portsmouth and Newcastle game at Fratton Park was delayed for half an hour by a fuse failure but the public imagination was captured by the spectacle. It all seemed quicker and more dramatic and what's more, clubs discovered a new source of income with midweek evening fixtures. Floodlights added a theatrical dimension to football. These days Old Trafford is even referred to as the 'Theatre of Dreams'.

But back to Carlisle who, ironically have a small place in football history because of floodlights. Tom Clish, a Wheatley Hill lad who kept goal for Darlington from 1955-57, informed me that he had appeared in the very first FA Cup-tie to be played under lights in the competition proper. The first round replay between Carlisle and Darlington in 1955 was staged at Brunton Park with a second goalless draw the result. Darlington was the eventual winner in a second, floodlit replay at St. James' Park, Newcastle. Incidentally, Tom Clish turned out 52 times for Darlington before thinking better of it and joining the police for more money and a pension. Who says goalkeepers are mad?

The 'G' Team

	Seasons	Apps	Goals	Source
Eric Gates (F)				
Ferryhill, 28 June 1955 E-2				
Ipswich Town	1973-84	296	73	APP
Sunderland	1985-89	181	43	TR
Carlisle Utd	1990	38	8	TR

Interviewed June 1999

Eric Gates had the good fortune to be at Ipswich Town during the most successful period of their history under the stewardship of one of Britain's great post-war managers, Bobby Robson. Born in Ferryhill but schooled and brought up in Staindrop and Barnard Castle, he was spotted playing for Bishop Auckland Boys by the famous Ipswich scouting system. It was a tough and ruthless selection process that left Eric hopelessly homesick, yet determined to realise his dream. But as Eric himself says, "the dream came true." He turned out to be one of a band of creative yet explosive ball players from that era like Curry, Kember, Hudson and Bowles who you can't believe have not been recognised with more caps for their country. Though Eric's game was in a more advanced position than that particular quartet of talent.

He played with and against the best of his generation both at club level and in the two full internationals in which he appeared, against Norway and Romania. However, the privilege he felt at representing his country was matched by the devastation of making the squad of 26 for the 1982 World Cup finals in Spain only to be omitted from the final 22 by Ron Greenwood. Of the many great players he encountered, Kevin Beattie his Ipswich colleague and Johan Cruyff, an opponent in European competition, were the most memorable. Bobby Robson had likened Beattie to the late Busby Babe Duncan Edwards such was his dominating presence. Cruyff was simply a footballing legend who introduced a new vocabulary of skills to the game. To play against Cruyff and his Barcelona team-mates was just another magic moment in the Gates dreamworld.

But Ipswich was his great love. A family club, run by the Cobbalds, owners of a local brewery, which reached the heights and competed with the best under Bobby Robson. They won the FA Cup in 1977-78, the UEFA Cup in 1980-81, were runners-up in the First Division in 1980-81 and competed in Europe for a decade. Four happy seasons followed at Sunderland. Ironic since he'd been a huge Middlesbrough fan as a youngster, watching brother Bill from the terrraces. Then the final chapter in a great career was played out at Carlisle United in 1990 where this football fan saw many of his performances, but as he readily admits, he had a fairly unhappy time. It's a long way from The Nou Camp to Brunton Park.

Eric, as one of 'The Three Legends', is now an established soccer pundit in the media-dominated modern game. Metro Radio, Tyne Tees Television and the Sunderland Echo keep the wolves from the door and after dinner speaking puts jam on the table. He still loves the game, though his brief spell coaching at Hartlepool in the early '90's, where staff were lucky to be paid at all, did nothing to lure him into management. Now he purrs over players like Kinkladze, Ginola and the young Ipswich-bred talent, Kieran Dyer whilst occasionally turning out in charity games. But he regrets that in an obscenely money orientated game, it's unlikely that another small town club like that at Portman Road will ever achieve the consistent level of success that they enjoyed.

	Seasons	Apps	Goals	Source
William Gates (CH)				
Ferryhill, 8 May 1944 E Yth				
Middlesbrough	1961-73	233	12	JNRS

Bill Gates was your archetypal one-club man. Eleven years the senior of brother Eric, he was the complete opposite as a player. He was a solid centre-half who plied his trade in the Second and Third Divisions with a club who couldn't quite make it to the top floor of the English game and seemed to be the perpetual under-achievers of the modern era. He had been captain of the England Youth Team and made his Boro debut the week before his seventeenth birthday, the first of over 300 first team appearances. His popularity with the Boro fans was underlined when nearly 32,000 turned up for his testimonial against champions Leeds at Ayresome Park in May 1974. It earned him a £16,000 golden handshake and he was released from his contract two months later.

However, Bill knew there was more to life than football so he had studied accountancy to help make his way after the legs had gone. He famously spotted the potential for growth in the leisurewear market and opened his first sports shop in his testimonial year. It was sold to Monument Sports in 1987 for a cool £4.4 million affording Bill the luxury of going into tax exile in The Cayman Isles. He later employed his business acumen in America where he saw the value of soccer franchising in Boston amongst other places. If good timing is necessary in sport it is also the case in business. He knew the World Cup was coming to The States in 1994 and his second fortune was duly made on the back of a soccer boom. His two sons still run soccer schools in New England.

Nowadays, he still resides in exile with his wife Judith whom he married at seventeen. They live in a £1.5 million beachside apartment where Bill plays tennis, swims and generally enjoys life. However, his business juices recently started to flow again when he became a major shareholder in the luxurious Whitworth Hall Hotel near Spennymoor. But his tax exile status means he's only allowed three months a year back in Blighty, so for the other nine months its world travel and Caribbean paradise for the Gateses. It's a life they've managed to come to terms with!

Bill Gates (far left) after playing golf with old Boro colleagues in 1998 – it's what ex-footballers do.
Can you name the others? Answer on page 118

	Seasons	Apps	Goals	Source
Martin Gray (M)				
Sedgefield, 17 August 1971				
Sunderland	1991-95	64	1	YT
Aldershot	1990	5	0	L
Fulham	1995	6	0	L
Oxford Utd	1995-99	121	4	TR
Darlington	1999-2000	66	0	TR

Interviewed March 2002

June 1999 saw Martin Gray return to his native North-East with a free move from Oxford to Darlington. Multi millionaire businessman, George Reynolds bought the club at the end of the 1998-99 season promising a new 25,000 all-seater stadium and an ambition to succeed never before encountered by Quakers fans. Martin had been a valuable squad player at Sunderland without quite claiming a regular first team spot during his period at Roker Park and in transfer deadline week of the 1995-96 season moved to the Manor Ground at Oxford for £100,000.

Martin Gray as a Sunderland aspirant

His League debut had come on loan at Aldershot where he faced Paul Ward in the Scunthorpe midfield. Paul had been kind enough to show him around the ground before the match then proceeded to kick the young debutant out of the match by way of welcome to the professional game. He played four more times before returning to Roker Park where he made his Sunderland League debut the following season against Cambridge at the Abbey Stadium in the Second Division. As with many players, this represented a career highlight - the first step onto the big stage.

Martin, a product of Sedgefield 'Comp', had been an apprentice joiner with the local council whilst playing for Ferryhill in the Northern League. He was captain of the Durham County under 18s when they won the County Championship, an immensely proud moment in a fledgling career. This led to a place at Roker Park as a Youth Trainee under Dennis Smith who would later take him to Oxford where, as captain, he had the happiest and most sustained phase of first team action in his career. Nevertheless, his four seasons in contention at Sunderland saw action in the First and Second Divisions, when the first was the top flight, and brought him into contact with many great players. Paul Bracewell, Kevin Ball and Peter Davenport impressed as team-mates but it was in his Oxford incarnation that he encountered the greatest - Gazza. In an end of season canter at the Riverside, Middlesbrough was hosting the Manor Ground team and the centre of midfield was all about Gray v Gascoigne. It was 1998 and Gazza was soon to be dumped out of the World Cup squad but he was great fun. Martin had "kicked him all over the pitch" and Gazza decided to use his shirt to stop the irritation. "You can have the shirt if you F...Off". Martin eased up and now has the prized shirt as part of a proud collection that also includes those of Zola and Di Matteo. In fact Zola had posted his shirt to Martin after forgetting to give it to him after agreeing to a post-match swap. The Italian was a true gentleman.

Back at Sunderland, Martin scored the first of his five career League goals against Portsmouth infront of The Fulwell End. He remembers it well - 'a crushing left-footer' after a long distance dash from the back and a nifty one-two with Peter Davenport. However, come 1995 first-team opportunities were diminishing and as Peter Reid established himself Martin was loaned out to Fulham as his Sunderland career ended and Oxford beckoned. He'd been somewhat unfortunate at Roker Park, missing out on a medal in the promotion season of 1995/96, only one appearance short of a gong and in 1992 he was injured as Malcolm Crosby's team reached the FA Cup Final. However, he had three days in London on the club and was able to take part in the open-top bus ride when the team returned, still heroes in defeat.

The same Martin on hearing that Faustino Asprilla is to sign for Darlington (Photo: Paul Kingston)

So, to the return of the native. Back in the region at the ambitious, turbulent but never-dull Darlington, Martin became club captain. He had been offered 'great money' to be part of the Reynolds revolution and in two seasons saw action at Wembley in the Third Division play-off final, defeat and the end of his playing career - a back injury sustained at Chesterfield eventually leading to a prolapsed disc, fused vertebrae and his worst moment in the game when the consultant said it was stop or be crippled. Still, good things often come from adversity. The Wembley game was the last domestic encounter in the old stadium and Martin pinched a souvenir bog-roll holder from the changing rooms; there aren't too many of those in Trimdon, where he now lives. The misery of having to quit playing at thirty saw the beginning of his coaching and managerial career with appointment to the Youth Team Manager's position. Getting three kids into the first team has quickly established his reputation at this discipline and he now nurtures an ambition to become a top-flight manager. He's doing the right things like taking the UEFA coaching badges and the early plaudits suggest he's made a seamless transition to the tracksuit.

His father once said that he would watch every one of his matches because in football, 'every game could be your last'. It's a maxim that speaks of living for the day and making the most of life's opportunities. I suspect Martin will never forget it.

is for Gentlemen

There is an anonymous but well-known quotation, which asserts that:

 "Football is a gentleman's game played by hooligans, and rugby a hooligan's game played by gentlemen."

I suspect this was a euphemism for 'an upper class pastime played by working class men', since by the late 19th century the game had largely been adopted and refined by the universities, officer establishment and public schools. However, the well meaning amateurs were not well organized and the game was in a mess with fixtures cancelled at a whim, often with little or no notice and spectators turning up to deserted grounds. It took a Scottish businessman, William McGregor, in Birmingham to resolve the problem by effectively forming the Football League when he invited eleven other clubs to join his beloved Aston Villa in a professional league based on a home and away fixture list. And so it was in 1888 that working men led by businessmen put two fingers up to the so-called gentlemen of the amateur game.

It is interesting, however, how the word 'gentleman' still has deep meaning within the game. Over a hundred years since football changed so dramatically and was claimed back by the working classes a player could still be penalised for 'ungentlemanly conduct'. Officially, that phrase was altered to 'unsporting conduct' a few years ago but somehow it has remained in the football vocabulary as a reminder that sportsmanship and fair play are central to the game.

In my personal experience the word has also been used as a term of admonishment. Imagine the upright, stiff-backed running style of Paul Madeley of the great 1970's Leeds team. Younger sports fans might like to reference the 400 metre phenomenon Michael Johnson. Now, I hesitate to bracket myself with these two supreme sportsmen but I do have a similar posture when in full flight. I recall vividly during one practice match at junior school being confused by the criticism, "Chaytor, you're running like a gentleman!" What was so bad about that?

The comment came from my teacher Tommy Hoban and I think it is appropriate to mention two other incidents involving him, which have always remained with me. Firstly there was the occasion when our captain, Terry McCann was upended by a wild challenge. I still recall the words; "On your feet Boy!" resounding around the field before his body had hit the ground. Secondly, while leading 10-0 against Shotton Junior School with half their team in tears and the fathers shaking their heads in embarrassment, Tommy blew the final whistle with twenty minutes still to play.

Perhaps what he was trying to say through these two incidents was that sport is about striving and competing. It is about fulfilling potential and yes, winning and losing but always with grace and dignity. It is not about humiliation. Perhaps this is sportsmanship. Perhaps this is what those who drew up the simple rules of football meant by playing like a gentleman. So long as you don't run like one.

KNOTTY HILL GOLF CENTRE
SEDGEFIELD

Telephone: (01740) 620320
Fax: (01740) 622227

PRIVATELY OWNED GOLF COMPLEX

OPEN DAILY
7.00 a.m. to 9.00 p.m.

✦ Indoor Golf Academy

✦ Tution Range

✦ High quality floodlit driving ranges

✦ Target golf and open grass tee area

✦ Practice bunker and putting greens

✦ Golf club hire available

✦ Tuition by appointment

✦ Fitness Studio

Princes Course
18 Holes (par 72)
Set in rolling parkland

Bishops Course
18 Holes (par 70)
A challenge for the experienced golfer

The 'H' Team

	Seasons	Apps	Goals	Source
Garry Haire (W)				
Sedgefield, 24 July 1963				
Oxford Utd	1981	0	0	APP
Bradford City	1983-84	49	13	Whitley Bay
Darlington	1984-85	25	2	TR
Rochdale	1985	3	0	L

Interviewed April 2000

Garry Haire's football career was nothing if not varied and eventful. Known as a winger, he actually preferred playing centre-forward but originally started life as a goalkeeper good enough to have trials for Newcastle, Wolves and Arsenal. At five feet eight inches he was never likely to succeed between the posts but he was quick, direct and skilful hence his opportunity came in the outfield.

Born in the Hardwick maternity hospital, Sedgefield, his childhood memories are of home in Bowburn. It was after leaving school at sixteen that he was taken on by Nottingham Forest a year after their first European Cup triumph. It wasn't a happy time. He found it difficult to fit in and always felt that local boy Steve Hodge received greater attention from coaches Liam O'Kane and Ron Fenton. The great Mr. Clough was rarely seen but it was clear that even the first-teamers were in awe of him. Garry soon returned to the North-East with Whitley Bay in the Northern League and after only five games was spotted by Oxford United under ex Man

Garry Haire sells a dummy to a two-headed, mutant Sheffield United defender at Bramhall Lane in 1983

Utd full-back, Ian Greaves. However, after a change of manager, new man Jim Smith released Garry even though he had been the top scorer in the reserves. Short of cash, Smith had little choice and later, in programme notes for a Bradford v Oxford clash when Garry was at Valley Parade, he admitted it was a mistake to let him go. It was soon back to Whitley Bay and a trial for Newcastle with Arthur Cox in charge. Alas, there was no joy for him at St. James' Park as they entered the Kevin Keegan era but a subsequent trial with Bradford City landed the long awaited contract and two seasons of Third Division football under Trevor Cherry and Terry Yorath - a very effective managerial team according to Garry. Unfortunately, the signing of John Hendrie in the second season came as Garry was suspended and he never regained his first team position. As a consequence he transferred to Darlington half way through the season, missing Bradford's eventual promotion but joining in the fun as Darlington were promoted to Division Three.

His relationship with the manager, Cyril Knowles, was not as it might have been and after being played out of position on a number of occasions, he began to fade from the picture. A loan spell with Fourth Division Rochdale, under Sunderland Cup Final hero, Vic Halom followed. He enjoyed his brief spell at Spotland. He liked Halom but again suffered from a manager's lack of cash and returned to Feethams. A possible move to Belgium stalled when Knowles demanded a fee, and a loan to Conference team, Scarborough proved fruitless. Darlington paid up his contract at the end of 1985-86 and he returned once again to Whitley Bay where he netted a bagful of goals.

A bad cartilage and ligament injury sustained at Gretna effectively ended his career at the age of twenty-five. He has hardly played since. Now he's a single parent to three children working for a circuit systems company in Newcastle. Unsurprisingly, he is rather preoccupied with domestic responsibilities. However, he enjoys watching football, particularly the likes of Roy Keane and David Ginola - "…he makes the game look so easy". He also helps run an under 12's team containing Haire Junior. After so many bad breaks you might imagine that there would be some bitterness, but no. He has no regrets and was simply thrilled to play the game to a professional standard. He particularly remembers his League debut versus Orient and was proud to play with the likes of Stuart McCall and Mark Wright whilst having the great honour of opposing Beardsley and Waddle in a League Cup match for Bradford and one of his personal favourites, Brian Marwood.

The career may have been short lived but at least he got the opportunity to rub shin pads with some of his heroes. And that's worth telling the grandkids.

	Seasons	Apps	Goals	Source
John Heaviside (LB) Ferryhill, 7 October 1943 Darlington (Am)	1963	2	0	Bishop Middleham

Interviewed May 2000

John Heaviside was associated with Darlington for three seasons from 1962-63 to 1964-65 but spent most of that time appearing for the reserve team as an amateur. He had been spotted by one of Eddie Carr's scouts playing for Bishop Middleham and used to catch the bus to Feethams to turn out for the second eleven for whom he played in almost every position. Around the same time Darlington signed George McGeachie, an outside-left from Dundee who had appeared in a European Cup semi-final with the Dens Park team the previous season. He was working for ICI and appearing as a part time pro' for Darlington. Both players had the dubious distinction of representing Darlington in the 0-10 defeat by Doncaster on 25th January 1964. It was McGeachie's debut, John's second and last League appearance and is still Darlington's record League defeat.

His debut and only other League appearance was in the previous match, a 1-2 away defeat at Lincoln City. As an amateur, he was working full time in the building trade and playing football with Darlington whenever he got the opportunity. However, those opportunities dried up when Lol Morgan replaced Eddie Carr so he returned to the non-league game with Stanley, Spennymoor and Blue Star in the Northern League. He was later to manage Spennymoor but left in 1985 feeling that money was beginning to spoil local football.

Nowadays he watches the odd live match at Sunderland and earns a living in the selling trade. He lost a bit of interest in the game because of the saturation coverage on TV but now he's helping to form a new team in Ferryhill, so perhaps some of the old enthusiasm is returning.

	Seasons	Apps	Goals	Source
Maurice Hilton (FB)				
Trimdon, 14 March 1979				
Doncaster Rovers	1997	10	0	YT

Trimdon's Maurice Hilton never actually signed professionally for Doncaster Rovers but played ten League games for the Belle Vue club in season 1997/98 as a youth trainee. His misfortune was to be with the club in the year they finished bottom of the Football League and were relegated to The Conference. After a seventy-five year run, Doncaster Rovers was replaced by Yorkshire neighbours, Halifax. His debut had come in a 1-2 defeat at Lincoln City in a season when youth team players were plunged into the first team to reduce the cost of the playing staff - youth team members didn't receive appearance money. Full-time professionals were off-loaded with the club in administration and a number of non-league players signed to supplement the youngsters. Businessman, Ken Richardson had taken over the club and was hailed as the saviour who would bring a new stadium and glory to the club. However, the council refused to deal with him and after a 'dodgy' incident, which saw the stand destroyed by arson, he was imprisoned. Manager, Mark Weaver lasted until the death knell sounded and inevitable relegation followed the worst period in Doncaster's history. Maurice Hilton left along with many others at the end of the season, his League career over at barely eighteen.

	Seasons	Apps	Goals	Source
David Hockaday (W/FB)				
Sedgefield, 9 November 1957				
Blackpool	1976-82	147	24	Billingham Synthonia
Swindon Town	1983-90	245	7	TR
Hull City	1990-91	72	2	TR
Stoke City	1992	7	0	L
Shrewsbury Town	1993-94	48	0	TR

Interviewed July 1999

Born in Sedgefield but brought up in Billingham, David Hockaday was that rare animal, a footballer with an academic background. However, after gaining four 'A' levels, he chose not to further his education but take up the challenge of a career in the professional game. It was a career that spanned 17 years in the Second, Third and Fourth Divisions with perhaps the cruelest blow coming in 1989-90 when Swindon outclassed Sunderland to win the Second Division play-off final at Wembley 1-0, only to have the FA relegate Swindon and promote Sunderland following an investigation into illegal payments at The County Ground. David was on the bench for that game but he, like the rest of the players, was utterly devastated by the FA ruling.

He had been spotted playing for Billingham Synthonia and was tempted away to Blackpool where he appeared in almost 150 League games for the likes of Stan Ternent, Bob Stokoe, Allan Brown and Alan Ball. They were relegated from Third Division in 1980-81 but he had the great pleasure of playing alongside Mike Summerbee, Willie Morgan and Alan Ball whom he describes as having 'frightening enthusiasm for the game'.

It was, however, with Swindon Town that he enjoyed the greatest highlights of his career under Lou Macari and Ossie Ardilles. They were promoted as runaway Division Four champions in 1986 with 102 points then to the Second Division the following season. Then came the calamitous end to the 1989-90 campaign when they were promoted to the First Division on the field of play then relegated weeks later by an FA ruling. And thereby hangs David's greatest regret, that he was robbed of the opportunity to play at the highest level by a governing body who seemed intent on making an example of a small club for sins that are doubtless committed on a much grander scale by their more wealthy cousins.

A spell on loan to Stoke under his old boss, Lou Macari, saw David help City to the Second Division (old Third) championship. His final move to Shrewsbury yielded another promotion from the Third Division (old Fourth) to round off a roller-coaster playing career including 519 League appearances and no fewer than seven promotions and relegations. There followed a spell playing in the DR. Martens League for Cirencester where he now runs the youth team and a top football academy in his joint role as lecturer in Sport and Recreation at Cirencester College and Director of the Academy.

He is passionate about his latest role developing football talent for the future, having fashioned an academy so successful it has won the ESFA (English Schools) and British Colleges championships for the past three years and is being looked upon by many professional clubs as a model of good practice. His philosophy is to put the fun back into football and to promote expression amongst his charges. Remove the pressure from players and you will get results. He believes that one of the fundamental problems with the pro' game is that it is riddled with fear. The fear of defeat and failure. He still watches the game and follows the results of his old teams, particularly Swindon. Indeed, he remains close friends with Dave Bamber, Colin Calderwood and Jimmy Quinn and looks back with gratitude on the opportunities offered by Lou Macari and the formative experiences gained under his management.

But his future lies with coaching and it is to the future he looks with the new talent emerging from Cirencester Academy. Listen out for the name Andy Manfell, recently taken on by Aston Villa. He is David Hockaday's first 'tip for the top.'

	Seasons	Apps	Goals	Source
John Hope (G)				
Shildon, 30 March 1949				
Darlington	1964-68	14	0	APP
Newcastle Utd	1968	1	0	TR
Sheffield Utd	1970-73	63	0	TR
Hartlepool Utd	1975	23	0	R

John Hope's twelve-year career in the Football League included the taste of success at Sheffield Utd in 1971 when The Blades were promoted to Division One as runners-up to Leicester City. He stayed with the club until 1975, enjoying three seasons in the top flight under managers Johnny Harris and Ken Furphy. He had begun his career as an apprentice at Feethams, making fourteen appearances for Darlington over five seasons. His League debut had been in a 0-2 home defeat to Crewe Alexander when he deputised for Jimmy O'Neill. He was just sixteen years and 265 days.

However, John Hope's claim to fame is actually recorded in the Guinness Book of Football Facts and Figures. Consider this sequence of events. After playing for Darlington in the Third Division relegation season of 1966-67 John turned out a further four times for The Quakers in the Fourth Division the following year. Before he could play a fifth time, he was snapped up by Newcastle Utd of the First Division for whom he pulled on the goalkeeper's jersey just once. He next appeared in the League at Sheffield Utd in the Second Division promotion team of 1970-71. This meant that from his last game for Darlington in the Third Division to the first for Sheffield in the Second, he had played in every division of the League within the space of seven games.

	Seasons	Apps	Goals	Source
John Hornsby (OL)				
Ferryhill, 3 August 1945				
Colchester Utd	1965	11	1	Evenwood Town

Interviewed June 1999

John Hornsby's brief League career may never have happened had it not been for an electrician friend of his working on a contract in Colchester who pestered United's manager Neil Franklin to give John a trial. Franklin gave in, John had his trial and impressed so much he was offered a full time contract on £20 per week, doubling his wages as a time-served welder. In 1964-65 he played reserve team football in the Combination League with teams like Chelsea and Spurs so had the opportunity to test himself against people such as Les Allen and George Graham. They also won the Essex Professional Cup with a promising young team. However, in the 1965-66 pre-season he was injured playing against Ipswich Town. He made his debut versus Port Vale and also started the second match at home to Scunthorpe but the injury had not been given enough time to heal and he missed the following six games. This was to be the recurring theme of the season, in and out with injuries.

John Hornsby doesn't look convinced by the Colchester strip in 1965 – "I should have been the fifth Beatle"

Colchester's successful Easter programme was John's highlight with an unbeaten run against Luton, Torquay and Port Vale including his only League goal in the latter match. This was the springboard to promotion, which was achieved on the last day of the season. John still remembers manager Franklin dashing excitedly back into the changing room after the drawn game at Newport to tell them that other results had gone their way. They were fourth behind Doncaster, Darlington and Torquay, pipping Tranmere and Luton on goal average. Alas, that was the end. He was given a free transfer and moved back north, back to welding and a spell at South Shields to keep him in touch with the game.

H is for Hand-shake

According to people who study these things, there are fourteen major types of body contact which are known as tie-signs and represent the most common social intimacies. They include amongst others, the most formal of hand-shakes, full embraces, kissing and what is known as the 'mock attack' whereby one person will push, grab, squeeze or 'hair-ruffle' another in the knowledge that they will not be hurt and will indeed accept the gestures as affectionate.

The hand-shake is also used as a 'salutation display' demonstrating that we mean someone well or at least we mean them no harm. In modern man it has also evolved into a means of greeting or saying farewell to someone.

So what do you suppose is going through the minds of football folk in the various situations you would expect to find them shaking hands?

Two captains shake hands with arm's length formality at the toss-up before the whistle and wish each other a 'good game mate'. Do they really hope the opposition performs well or are they really thinking 'we've got plans to take you out in the first minute pal'?

The Queen meets the teams before The Cup Final and asks the odd obligatory question of the famous one and the English one as each player, in turn simultaneously shakes and nods deferentially. This should be a salutation display but she is probably thinking 'One can't take any more of this populist mingling.' And they are probably thinking, 'I'm a republican Ma'am.'

Two managers indulge in an 'amplified' hand-shake after a particularly bruising encounter and presumably utter either 'well done son' or 'hard luck mate'. Have you noticed how they always place the non-shaking hand behind the neck of the other in a semi-embrace that would normally denote a growing warmth or affection (Kevin Keegan is a particularly fine exponent)? Warm and affectionate? I think not.

Then there is the goal celebration, which in days of yore would often be a manly hand-shake or at moments of high excitement, a pat on the back. What has gone wrong? A goal celebration in the modern age can be anything from a choreographed performance of some made-up dance to a frenzied heap of bodies kissing, hugging, grabbing, hair-ruffling, embracing and whatever comes naturally.

It is at this point that I am reminded that there are a total of 457 different types of body contact which include specialized touches used by people like priests, doctors and hairdressers and the highly intimate, normally exercised in private. From the Old Etonian hand-shake at number one, the modern footballer must have progressed to somewhere around number 360 and is still looking for new ways to celebrate. It's worrying really.

not all business support agencies are the same

To find out why and how we can help your business perform better, contact...

I is for Isotonic Drink

The 'I' Team

There is no League player from the Sedgefield area whose name begins with I. However, classic 'I' names from elsewhere include the fabulous Cecil 'Cess' Irwin of Sunderland fame and the current day Mustafa 'Muzzy' Izzet. Could you ever forget footballers called Cecil and Muzzy?

Have you ever stopped to consider the importance of the intake of fluid within the game of football? This is not just an issue for the performer but also the spectator and others associated with the game. The whole process of playing and watching the football is punctuated by refreshments taken at different times for different purposes and develops into a kind of ritualistic behaviour repeated week after week by the participants.

Take an average, traditional football fan. He will meet his mates an hour or two before a game for a pint of ale to get in the mood for the afternoon's entertainment. Once in the ground he may or may not, depending on the length of the queue, the capacity of the bladder and the ambient temperature, have another pint or Bovril (which these days is nearly always Oxo). Half time will usually be Bovril accompanied by a meat pie, pasty or a burger always wrapped in one sliver of grease proof paper or a serviette the size of a square of toilet roll. The end of the game is usually home or a pint depending on the domestic situation of the individual.

The above routine was roughly the same for Chelsea players in the sixties and seventies.

The average, traditional player would build himself up with sophisticated concoctions like milk and would be welcomed by the half time cup of tea, heavily sweetened for energy. I have it on good authority, however, that this was occasionally accompanied by something to 'pep them up', whatever that may have meant. After the game most right-minded players would have a few pints to celebrate victory or drown the sorrows of defeat.

Special victories will always bring out the old favourite, bubbly. Champagne is of course the staple celebratory bottle for most sports though most of it is showered rather than consumed. Drinking from the victory cup is, however, one of the great pleasures in sport.

Now, consider if you will, the modern game. The athlete (for that's what footballers are these days) is bombarded by all manner of food-drinks designed to help develop the body and aid performance. Much has been written about creatine, a naturally occurring substance that can be added to drinks to enable the performer to train harder and for longer so developing greater strength and stamina. It's legal but many believe it has unacceptable risks and side effects. However, the best of all is the 'isotonic drink' as advertised by John Barnes kicking a Lucozade can into a waste bin. In my day, Lucozade used to be a bottle of sugared water wrapped in a mysterious golden cellophane that you were supposed to put beside your bed when you were poorly. Now it's an isotonic drink. In physiological terms, isotonic means 'of equal tension', normally referring to two or more muscles. So now we're told that sugared water can replenish your body fluids and it is 'in balance with your body'. It used to be so simple, Bovril and beer for the fans, tea and beer for the players. Alright, I accept that things have to move on, but isotonic?

Is it just me or is someone trying to sell me something?

The 'J' Team

	Seasons	Apps	Goals	Source
Gordon Jones (FB)				
Sedgefield, 6 March 1943 E Yth/Eu23-9				
Middlesbrough	1960-72	462	4	JNRS
Darlington	1972-74	85	5	TR

Interviewed March 2000

Gordon Jones was a stalwart of the Middlesbrough team of the sixties that played all but one season in the Second Division, suffering the disappointment of relegation in 1965-66 under Raich Carter only to bounce straight back as runners-up to QPR in 1966-67 with new manager, Stan Anderson. He represented his country at youth and under-23 levels and made a total of 528 appearances for Middlesbrough, a post-war record and a figure bettered only by Tim Williamson in the history of the club. To cap it all, Gordon was the first Boro player to be granted a testimonial for his service to the club.

He was also a true Sedgefield lad, born and raised in the village, living for a period at Butterwick and also spending some of his childhood in the house that is now Minister's Restaurant. He left school at 15yrs and joined Boro as a member of the ground staff. However, his talent with the ball was evident and he made his first team debut in a League Cup tie at Cardiff aged only sixteen on the same day he was called up for the England youth team. He signed pro' forms at 17yrs and made his League debut versus Southampton at The Dell. He had actually travelled as reserve but Derek Stonehouse, the regular left-back, couldn't shake off a bout of the flu and Gordon was asked to fill his boots. Southampton has figured large in the career of Gordon Jones. Not only did his debut come against them but also his 200th appearance. To complete the coincidence, the Boro centenary match was played against Southampton in 1976 and Gordon was invited as a guest of the club.

Gordon Jones opens a Middlesbrough toy shop in 1968 while Leslie Crowther stands in the background rounding up an audience for Crackerjack

As Gordon's Middlesbrough career burgeoned, so did his international credentials. He was a regular in the Under 23 squad, making nine appearances for his country. Teammates included the West Ham trio of Moore, Peters and Hurst plus Brian Labone and goalkeeper Gordon West. Indeed many of the eventual World Cup winning squad were colleagues in an emerging Under 23 team. Sadly, luck deserted Gordon in 1965 when a broken foot kept him out of the international tour and many people feel that this ended his chances of being part of the squad for the 1966 tournament. He was never capped by his country again following the '66 triumph. However, he has fond memories of the international scene. Bobby Moore was "a great player but an ordinary lad who loved a pint." Ramsey, Billy Wright, Winterbottom, Geenwood and Mercer, a veritable who's who of the great managers of the era were all associated with the international set-up at the time. Though it was Stan Anderson in domestic football who impressed as much as anyone. He was a thoroughly decent man who had great tactical awareness and was unfortunate not to break into the big time with an entertaining Boro team. Big Jack Charlton eventually did it "…by putting up the shutters."

His Boro career continued successfully and often as team captain. He saw the emergence of some great young talent such as the legendary Brian Clough and the seventies stars Eric McMordie, John Hickton and Graeme Souness whom he regarded as Boro greats. However, it was Bill Harris the Welsh international inside-forward and wing-half whom he regarded as the best of them all. He served the club from 1953 to 1964 before departing for Bradford City. Opponents included Stanley Matthews whom he'd watched in the famous Matthews Cup Final of 1953 and who pulled a muscle after five minutes of an encounter between Stoke and Middlesbrough. He had just pushed the ball past Gordon and was off down the wing when the muscle went. Gordon could always say he played Matthews off the park. George Best was a direct opponent on five or six occasions, a "…great player and a great character." However, his true heroes were the players in the local leagues when he was a youngster. The Sedgefield St. Edmunds team was amongst those that inspired Gordon Jones to great things. Going on to play with and against some of the game's legends was a wonderful consequence of that inspiration.

In 1972 Gordon transferred to Darlington for the first of three seasons that would bring down the curtain on a long and distinguished career. He was assistant player-manager to Billy Horner for a period of time, thinking full time management may be the next move. However, he became disillusioned with the Feethams experience, kicked to bits by opponents and with a club that refused to initiate a proper youth policy. They had finished bottom of the League in 1972-73 and little progress had been made since. Frankly, he felt he was wasting his time and began to believe that moving to Darlington was the worst thing he had ever done. In 1975 he called it a day and went on to develop the newsagent business he had started whilst at Middlesbrough. He did some coaching with schools and also managed Crook Town for a while. Indeed, it was he who organized the famous India trip that saw Crook touring the great cricket grounds of the sub-continent performing before mammoth crowds and being feted as superstars.

Gordon still follows the Boro and is happy that they've achieved a measure of success in recent years. However, he is disappointed that the current team (under Robson) lacks flair and is be-devilled by poor tactics. Not enough youngsters are being given the opportunity to develop. He remains a fan though.

On the home front, he has backed off the business somewhat and is in remission after being told in 1998 that he has lymphatic leukemia. He is refreshingly philosophical about his illness, which he says is manageable and still allows him to live a full life. He talks with great admiration of his friend and ex colleague Willie Maddren who died from motor neurone disease in March 2000. Willie retained his spirit and a wicked sense of humour to the end. In the presence of this kind of courage it is difficult not to be inspired, to be positive about life.

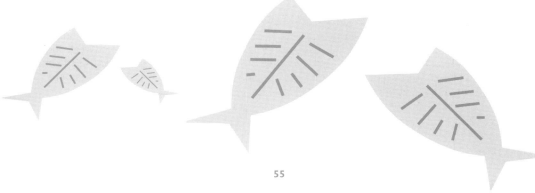

is for Justification

There are many times in life when we are asked to justify our actions or explain ourselves whether at home, in the workplace or for those with less conventional life-styles, in court. Sport is a field of activity in which participants and to an even greater extent managers and coaches, are often asked to justify or explain themselves. The manager's decision on team selection, the player's explanation for poor performance, the chairman's reason for lack of investment, the hooligan's excuse for anti-social behaviour.

The microscopic examination of football by the media in recent years has lead to post-match analysis which is almost forensic in its complexity and subjects the most trivial of incidents to a kind of trial. There are some classic cases of which we are all aware like Alex Ferguson's excuse for a poor first half performance by Manchester Utd being the new grey shirts they were wearing. Then there is the pathetic excuse for cheating which Diego Maradonna used claiming that the 'Hand of God' had scored against England as opposed to his own wayward mitt.

But the manager is probably under more under pressure than most to justify his decisions. Take Bobby Robson after refusing to announce his team to the press in advance of a World Cup qualifier with Sweden:

"Hitler didn't tell us when he was going to send over those doodle bugs, did he?"
I rather like the psychological diversion of immediately focusing the attention on another hate figure instead of the beleaguered manager himself.

Then there's Bobby Gould's justification of Wimbledon's roughhouse tactics:

"We're aggressive and we're competitive, but we can't all be Desert Orchids and loved by everyone." Here, Gould uses his favourite tactic of making such a bizarre analogy that everyone is left scratching their heads.

And what of the football fan, that lifeblood of the English game? A good example would be the Sunderland fan who, when challenged in court over his attack on a Charlton supporter, explained:

"He was skitting me, so I hit him." No apology or analogy here, just a rather disarming honesty which demonstrates the psychological trauma of being skitted.

But it's an ex-player and a respected commentator who combine to demonstrate the complex simplicity of football with a one-two that unintentionally asks the question, why should we require justification at all?

John Motson: "Well, Trevor, what does this substitution mean tactically?"

Trevor Brooking: "Well, Barnes has come off and Rocastle has come on."

The 'K' Team

	Seasons	Apps	Goals	Source
Frank Kirkup (OL)				
Spennymoor, 12 January 1939				
Blackburn Rovers	1957	0	0	Spennymoor Utd
Workington	1959-62	140	31	TR
Carlisle Utd	1962-64	76	15	TR
Notts County	1965	29	0	TR
Workington	1966	8	0	retirement

Interviewed July 1999

It was a 10-0 defeat of Spennymoor Juniors at the hands of Blackburn Juniors in the FA Youth Cup that propelled Frank Kirkup towards a ten-year career in the professional game. Frank must have been the only thing that shone in the Spennymoor performance at Ewood Park but it was enough to pursuade Johnny Carey to offer him a trial. After four visits to Rovers, Frank signed professional forms on his 18th birthday. He spent around two and a half seasons amongst stars like Ronnie Clayton and Roy Vernon but never quite made the first eleven. However, he had the honour of facing the Busby Babes in the Central League and recalls being thrashed 0-4 and 0-5 by the best in Britain.

His thirst for first team football was satisfied in 1959 by a transfer to Workington Town under the young Joe Harvey. He enjoyed almost four seasons at Borough Park and recalls training at the old Lonsdale ground with it's dog track and decaying stands. One of his clearest memories was a 0-1 defeat against Blackpool in the third round of the League Cup in 1961-62. His direct opponent that day was England's Jimmy Armfield, the best full-back he ever encountered. However, the arrival of Ken Furphy in 1962 saw the influx of a number of ex-Darlington players, including Davie Carr from Wheatley Hill, and Frank was edged out

Workington's Frank Kirkup struggles manfully under the weight of his own hair in 1966.
(Photo: Ivor Nicholas)

of the first team. Carlisle United stepped in to offer £3,500 plus a player, Geoff Martin, in order to take Frank to Brunton Park where he enjoyed three successful seasons, including a promotion from the Fourth Division to the Third in 1963-64. Carlisle were pipped to the title by Gillingham because of a marginally inferior goal average despite scoring almost twice as many goals, 113. Unfortunately, in those days only the champions received medals so there is no silverware on the Kirkup mantlepiece to mark the achievement. It was a good financial move for Frank though, his salary rising from £20 per week at Workington to £35 per wek with the abolition of the maximum wage.

By 1964 his form was not good at Brunton Park and he was offered a move to Notts County for a fee of £1,000. Alan Ashman sold him on but the move didn't suit him or his wife whom he'd married while in Cumbria. After one season he quit the game to return north where he used his

accumulated cash to buy a pub in Workington. Serving Matthew Brown ales in The Lamb Inn was to be his living from now on though he was briefly tempted back to Borough Park in 1966 by manager, George Ainsley. However, he couldn't afford the time away from the business and finally hung up his boots after only eight games. He never kicked a football again.

After splitting from his wife, he returned to Middlestone Moor in 1974 and spent some time working in insurance before re-marrying and moving to his present employers, furniture company NESF. He doesn't watch much football now, it's too boring, not direct enough. He was a flying winger with strict instructions to get past the full-back to the by-line and cross the ball for the centre forward. He feels that much of the excitement of direct play has been lost in the modern game. When pressed, however, he admits that Ronaldo is a decent turn.

He remains modest about his achievements, claiming to be a 'decent 3rd and 4th Division player'. But he is proud of his hat-trick for Carlisle versus Aldershot in 1964 and the three day period in 1960 when he scored two goals for Workington in a 3-0 defeat of Millwall on the Saturday and two more in the Monday night 5-3 defeat of Oldham Athletic at Boundary Park. He is also proud of the fact that he played fast and direct, the way it should be.

K is for Kipper

One of the great luxuries in life is the cooked breakfast. It's ironic that something so apparently mundane should be so, it's just that society has moved the goalposts. Gone are the days when the woman of the house would cook the man of the house a hearty first meal of the day to prepare him for a hard slog in one of the labour intensive industries that so sustained the old working class communities. Nowadays it is just as likely that the two of them will be setting off to some white collar desk job with none of the physical demands that used to be part and parcel of the working man's life. In addition to the change of lifestyle, there has been a revolution in the way we think about food and diet in this country. We are all so health conscious bombarded as we are by advice from every quarter on what to eat and what not to eat. Unfortunately, one of the main casualties of the modern approach to diet and lifestyle has been the great, British cooked breakfast.

Whenever I stay in a hotel in this country I always indulge myself. None of the usual fruit and fibre rubbish, it's scrambled eggs, mushrooms, bacon, sausage, fried bread, tea and toast. But occasionally I will vary the indulgence by having kippers. Herring cleaned, salted and smoked has become a rare treat. The very thought of steaming kippers spread out on a plate dripping with melted butter and powdered with pepper sets the lips-a-smacking.

Wonderful though they are, however, it is unusual to hear of smoked fish being used as currency but it has happened. Nicol Evans, who played his one and only League game for New Brighton in 1947, was the son of Hartlepool's reserve team manager Nick Evans senior. Father was a bit of a wheeler-dealer on the local scene, never happier than when talking football and one night while tasting a few with boys in the Vic at Wingate he struck up a conversation with the Wingate FC manager who had just come in. Now it so happens that Nick fancied one of his players (it's alright, you can say that in manager speak) and tried to get him to name his price. Anxious to close a deal quickly, he pressurised the Wingate boss into agreeing a sale. However, all Nick had on him was two quid, an old case ball and a box of kippers. I assume the kippers swung the deal. Legend has it that they were fried there and then on a shovel over the fire and eaten by way of celebration. Now that is what I call a bung.

Everything is not always as it seems in the world of football. There was much controversy in the 90's about transfer dealings, back-handers, inducements and back room deals. Nothing's changed really. However I can't imagine George Graham sitting in a Little Chef with a top player's agent discussing an intended transfer and when asked what it will take to swing the deal his personal demands extend no further than a box of Craster kippers.

Mind you, everything is not always as it seems in the world of kippers. Do you realise that herring are landed in West Cumbria, transported overland to Craster, salted and smoked in the village and sold as a local delicacy?

How's that for a scandal?

The 'L' Team

	Seasons	Apps	Goals	Source
Ian Larnach (F) Ferryhill, 10 July 1951 Darlington	1969	2	1	APP

Interviewed June 1999

Ian Larnach's first team appearances at Darlington were limited to two matches in the 1969-70 season when The Quakers finished third from bottom of the Football League ahead of Hartlepool and Bradford Park Avenue, who were subsequently replaced by Cambridge in the annual re-election vote. Both of his appearances were in defeats, 1-4 to Notts County and 1-3 to Aldershot. However, having scored once and played well on both occasions, he was mystified that he should be rejected so abruptly by manager Ray Yeoman. Indeed, the manager lost his own job at the end of a dismal campaign that had promised so much after just missing out on promotion the previous year.

Ian had spent three seasons at Darlington, two as an apprentice, after playing for Chilton and Aycliffe juniors and became particularly good friends with Peter Carr who went on to have a long career with Darlington, Carlisle and Hartlepool. However, with Ray Yeoman's policy of packing the team with old pros, Ian left the club and went on to feature for South Shields in the Northern Premier League. He did, infact return to Feethams in the early Eighties as reserve team coach under Billy Elliott, bringing in such players as Fred Barber, Kevin Stonehouse and Kevin Smith. But the long term future was away from football and he eventually worked for JT Atkinson before moving on to James Burrell Ltd where he is Business Development Officer. He reckons that football taught him much about management skills and dealing with people and that his involvement in the game had been a learning process that stood him in good stead for a new career.

Of course, as he sits at home in Spennymoor memories abound. He particularly recalls being substitute in a game against Leicester City in which the great Allan 'Sniffer' Clarke scored two effortless goals. He and Don Masson of Notts County were the two opponents who impressed him most. Now he enjoys the game as a spectator but worries about the grass roots and the misdirection of resources within the professional game. But as he says, "football is not a game any more."

	Seasons	Apps	Goals	Source
Michael Laverick (M) Trimdon, 13 March 1954				
Mansfield	1972-75	89	13	JNRS
Southend Utd	1976-78	110	18	TR
Huddersfield Town	1979-81	74	9	TR
York City	1981-82	41	6	TR
Huddersfield Town	1982	2	0	L

Interviewed March 2000

The declining coal industry of the 1950's and 60's North-East took Trimdon born Micky Laverick to the Nottinghamshire coalfields at the age of eight with his parents and hundreds of other miners who were looking for a future. As a consequence he is better remembered by those in the Midlands where he was raised. However, he is a Trimdon lad and a Sunderland fan to boot.

HARDWICK HALL
HOTEL

Situated in the beautiful County Durham countryside yet within easy reach of the A1 (M) and A19, Hardwick Hall provides a warm welcome to visitors who expects International standards in comfort and communications.

Bedrooms combine antique furnishings and high tech communications (ISDN and modem) including satellite, DVD, widescreen and plasma televisions.

Spacious bathrooms with huge walk in showers and deep baths offer accommodation of the highest standard, providing excellent views across the gardens and parkland of the Hardwick Country Park.

HARDWICK HALL HOTEL, SEDGEFIELD, COUNTY DURHAM. TS21 2EH
Telephone 01740 620253 Facsimile 01740 622771
www.hardwickhallhotel.co.uk   hardwickhall.sedgefield@virgin.net

He left school at fifteen to work in the local timber yard and was first noticed by Ian Greaves' Huddersfield who gave him a couple of trials but eventually declined to take him on. After a little time in the local leagues he was courted by Mansfield and was signed as a junior in 1970. He eventually signed amateur forms and played in the 'B' team and reserves in the North Midlands League. During this period Manchester City was also showing an interest so Micky used this as a bargaining chip to secure a six-month full-time contract. His £12 per week was half the wage he'd been receiving in his job at the timber yard but it was an opportunity too good to miss. In fact, he had the good fortune to appear in the County Cup Final versus Notts County with Don Masson, Willie Carlin et al at the end of the 1971-72 season. This was to be his first taste of success in a 3-0 victory. He was subsequently offered extended terms and enjoyed four years of first team involvement.

His League debut came in 1972 in the 1-0 home victory against Northampton. It was to be an 'in and out' year for the rookie pro' but he did enough to impress management and steadily established himself in the team. 1974-75 brought the first of three promotions Micky was to enjoy in his ten-year career when Mansfield became Fourth Division Champions under Dave Smith. However, 1975-76 brought a change of fortune when Smith was sacked and replaced by player-manager, Peter Morris who happened to play in Micky's position. He was moved up front unsuccessfully, leading to his eventual transfer to Southend - managed by Dave Smith. Mansfield was elevated to Division Two that season depriving him of consecutive promotion medals.

His time at Roots Hall was eventful and not without success. 1978-79 saw promotion to the Third Division under Dave Smith and on January 10th 1979 the team faced the all-conquering Liverpool in the FA Cup third round after disposing of Watford in the second. Over thirty one thousand fans, still a club record attendance, turned up for the home tie and witnessed a triumphant 0-0 draw. The replay was one of the highlights of Micky's career. The team travelled up to Liverpool for three days and prepared by training at Goodison Park. Whilst sitting in the Everton dressing room they were visited by, none other than Bill Shankley, who held the team in thrall as he sat and reminisced about Liverpool over a cup of tea. This was the team of Dalglish and Souness; two of the greatest opponents Micky ever faced. However, he also got the opportunity to measure himself against the Spurs stars on a regular basis since the two teams often played in pre-season friendlies. Glen Hoddle shone out like a beacon with "...class, ability and two great feet". He also became good pals with Peter Taylor who has now established himself as one of the country's top managers.

A move to Huddersfield in 1979 was rewarded by instant success with promotion to the Third Division; the third time Micky Laverick experienced that particular pleasure. However, following two final seasons in the League with York City in the Fourth Division, his mind turned to coaching. He did six years at the Nottingham Forest School of Excellence on a part-time basis whilst continuing to play for three seasons as a semi-pro' with Boston United in The Conference. Ironically, at this stage of his career came another high point with the 1985 FA Trophy final at Wembley Stadium. They lost 1-2 to Wealdstone in front of almost 40,000 fans with a youthful Vinnie Jones on the bench for the victorious team.

For the last sixteen years he's been in the prison service and continued to play some local league stuff until an arthritic hip got the better of him. Now he plays golf to a very useful nine handicap and prefers to watch his football from the comfort of his sitting room. He hates the language and aggression of the terraces and fears that youngsters are influenced by this fan hatred. However, he admires the skills of Giggs, Ginola and Keane in particular but regrets not having the opportunity to test himself at that level. He always seemed to excel against the better teams and so enjoyed playing on the bigger grounds. All in all, he has few regrets and thoroughly enjoyed the success he achieved. And after all, he got to play against his boyhood hero, Colin Todd. Another ambition achieved.

	Seasons	Apps	Goals	Source
Robert Laverick (OL)				
Trimdon, 11 June 1938 Eu19				
Chelsea	1956-57	7	0	JNRS
Everton	1958-59	22	6	TR
Brighton & H.A.	1960-61	63	20	TR
Coventry City	1962	4	0	TR

Interviewed February 2000

Bobby Laverick was a friend a schoolboy opponent of Kenny Chaytor in Trimdon in the early 1950's and very nearly followed him to Oldham Athletic as Owen Willoughby searched the area for fresh talent. However, Chelsea came in for him and the 1955 League Champions gave him his first taste of League football with his 1956 debut in a 2-3 defeat to West Brom at Stamford Bridge in front of over 30,000 fans. Unfortunately, his opportunities were few and far between as the effective understudy to England winger Frank Blunstone. These were some of the best of times at Chelsea though. Not only had they been League Champions in 1955 but every team from the juniors to the first team won their respective league that year. Such was the camaraderie at the club that they organised a huge celebration for everyone at the Park Lane Hotel and the juniors were feted every bit as much as the stars of Division One. This was the time of Greaves, Venables, Bonnetti, Tambling and England centre forward Roy Bentley. Wages were £18 per week with a £4 win bonus and the old Stamford Bridge terraces were in their pomp. The huge raking steps surrounding the field of play formed the characteristic oval shape that had bordered the greyhound track, which was still in use around the pitch, and

Bobby Laverick or is it Mark Lamarr before his Chelsea debut in 1956?

followed the line of the original athletics track. Bobby had to sweep that terrace with the other lucky juniors.

During these Chelsea years Bobby was also doing his national service based in Aldershot and with the medics in Dorset. However, much of his army life was an extension of his football career. Ted Drake, the Chelsea boss, would grease the palm of a particular Captain with tickets for top games. Army stripes could often be found being wined and dined in the Chelsea directors' box to ensure that Bobby Laverick was not unduly detained on army business. One of Bobby's best mates at the time was a certain Bobby Robson, already established in the Fulham team but rooming close by. They would often socialise together with a couple of the other young hopefuls, going to the pictures and coffee bars. Robson went on to become quite well known.

In 1958 Everton made Chelsea an offer for their understudy outside left. Bobby thinks the fee was around £20,000 but you didn't always know in those days. Players often didn't find out when offers were made let alone know the details of the deal. However, it was a great opportunity for Bobby who was assured of immediate first team football in Division One and manager John Carey was true to his word. However, bad fortune struck when he suffered a perforated appendix that laid him low for some time. He believes he came back too soon after the illness and performed poorly in a 1-6 away defeat to Wolves. A replacement winger brought in to cover for Bobby's illness was able to establish himself in the team and chances for the name Laverick to appear on the team-sheet were again limited.

The most fearsome opponent he ever faced was encountered in his days at Everton. The Goodison club would play Liverpool in pre-season friendlies aimed at raising money to pay for floodlighting. In one such fundraiser before 50,000 fans, Ronnie Moran kicked him off the park. It was like a war. Bobby's appeal to Moran's better nature - "Bloody hell Ronnie, it's only a friendly" - was met by savage grunts and another good kicking. He was a nutcase. Brian Labone, Bobby Collins and Alex Parker starred for Everton at the time and it was Collins who impressed Bobby as one of the best he had ever played alongside.

The appendix illness and subsequent loss of form effectively ended Bobby Laverick's top-flight career. He moved to Brighton in 1960 when Billy Lane signed him but they were unfortunately relegated to the Third Division in his second season after which he transferred to Coventry in the same division. He only got four outings at the Highfield Road club under the management of Jimmy Hill whom he rated as a nice enough bloke but who didn't seem to like the coaching. That was left to Alan Dicks and 'some Hungarian chap'. Hill obviously wanted some of the great Magyar talent to rub off onto Coventry. Bobby remembers a sign that the boss had plastered on the wall of the dressing room saying that 'the trouble with players is they get too much money'. Jimmy Hill hankering after the maximum wage?

Bobby's League days over, he played several seasons on the non-league scene at Corby, Kings Lynn and Ashford amongst others. Unfortunately he never got the desired move back north. Indeed, Ashford was where he eventually laid his hat and he's been there ever since. He worked on the railways for a while; the Ashford directors were clever at getting players jobs, and now works for a vending machine company. His two daughters and four grand children were brought up in the area so there is no reason to leave now. He still follows the game on Sky television and his spiritual home is still Stamford Bridge with memories of Ted Drake's secretary, Mrs. Metcalf, who would look after the young players, getting them tickets for the shows and writing to their parents with up-dates on progress. He regrets the appendix problem, which he believes effectively ended his chances of a prolonged career. However, he cherishes the highlight that was his under 19 cap for England in the same team as the great Duncan Edwards. The 2-3 defeat against Holland while he was still an amateur in 1955 was a moment to savour when he rubbed shoulders with the man who could have become England's greatest player. It's a memory worth hanging on to.

	Seasons	Apps	Goals	Source
Kenneth Lowe (M)				
Sedgefield, 6 November 1961E Semi Pro				
Hartlepool Utd	1981-83	54	3	APP
Scarborough	1987	4	0	Barrow
Barnet	1991-92	72	5	Barrow
Stoke City	1993	9	0	TR
Birmingham City	1993-95	21	3	TR
Carlisle Utd	1994	2	0	L
Hartlepool Utd	1995	13	3	L
Darlington (N/C)	1996-97	14	0	TR

Interviewed December 2001

Kenny Lowe's career has been one of the more varied and colourful of the professionals from Sedgefield District. To the above list of clubs can be added spells at non-league Barrow, Gateshead and Billingham and even a stint in Australia at Spearwood Dalmatinac, a largely Yugoslavian outfit based in Perth boasting a number of British ex-pats. He loved his time down under, describing the whole experience as 'party time.' On his return in 1986 he had a spell with Middlesbrough reserves before moving to Morecambe and then Barrow under ex-Gateshead manager, Ray Wilkie. It was during this period that he had a brief spell at Scarborough with Neil Warnock, resuming a League career that had begun at Hartlepool where he had been a junior from 1978. His next move took him to Conference side, Barnet where the club enjoyed promotions to the Fourth Division of the Football League and then to the Third. It was here that he encountered Barry Fry, a manager for whom he has the greatest admiration, and the larger-than-life chairman, Stan Flashman. It was a clash of two immense characters and they were even known to brawl on the changing room floor after falling-out. All the stories about the volatile relationship were true. There was never a dull moment with Barry and Stan. Kenny even recalls the time when he read on teletext that he, along with the club skipper, had been sacked by the club. Both chairman and manager blamed the other for putting out the story. But Ken is pretty sure that it was Fry who had been the culprit, taking a calculated gamble to embarrass the chairman into paying the players' wages that had been frozen by the cash-strapped club. Fry, unpredictable and irrepressible, was and remains a players' man. He signed Kenny for Barnet and Birmingham and 'improved my game 500%.'

Kenny's has been a patch-work career littered with success and a penchant for 'moving on.' He's been picked for the Third Division in the PFA select team, turned out for the England semi-professional side, won an FA Trophy Winner's medal at Wembley with Barrow and had two promotions with Barnet. He finally came to rest at Darlington, playing on a week-to-week basis for friend David Hodgson whom he regards as a top- notch manager who must surely return to the game if he feels the urge. However, he's a successful businessman and players agent and hardly needs the cash. As for Ken - he had a spell at Gateshead before taking on the managerial role at Barrow where things are going very well and, as we speak, he is happy to stay if offered a contract but other options are open to him. A return to Australia is not out of the question.

But there's more than football in his life. Having left school at 16 he became an apprentice fitter and pipe welder at ICI while playing part-time for Hartlepool. In fact it was only with his transfer to Stoke City that he finally became a full-time pro'. He also found time to complete a five-year BEng degree course sponsored by the petro-chemical firm for whom he was working. So, Kenny Lowe is no ordinary footballer and he has managed to save enough money along the way to have a house built on Sir John Hall's Wynyard estate where ordinary footballers like Kevin Keegan and Alan Shearer have lived.

Just shows you what a degree in engineering can do.

Kenny Lowe pulls out of yet another challenge for Hartlepool in 1995 (Photo: Hartlepool Mail)

is for Losing

In all sport, winning is the aim.

Striving to win is the essence of competition and the focus of sporting endeavour. Without it, the games we play would simply be physical performance and cease to be regarded as sport. Some managers, coaches and participants openly regard winning as the only thing of any consequence but unfortunately they have missed the point. Losing is far more important. The ability to lose and still remain motivated and competitive is what really defines sport. If those who have not won simply faded from the scene, sport would die. For every team that wins a competition there are scores more that have not. For every boy who achieves the dream of playing professional football there are hundreds who failed to make the grade, defeated by the weight of their own ambitions. It is true that achieving victory against the opposition does not exclusively define winning. It is just as valid to measure ourselves against what we believe is our own potential. However, in either case, how would we reach that ultimate goal if we did not learn from failure or defeat?

It is perhaps this understanding of the role of losing that makes the British so good at it. It is perhaps our empathy with the loser that ensures the runner-up is often celebrated more than the victor. Witness the scenes when Tim Henman reaches a quarter or semi-final at Wimbledon, when Damon Hill came second in the F1 World Championship or Frank Bruno was beaten up in another attempt at the World Heavy Weight title. We vote them BBC Sports Personality of the Year.

In fact, some sportsmen and sporting

teams are actually defined by their defeats or the manner of their losing. Some have known little else. The most famous of these is perhaps Eddie 'The Eagle' Edwards who was practically a music hall joke as the worst ski jumper in Olympic history, yet he became a kind of national hero, the like of which would simply not be tolerated in Germany or America. But in his own mind Eddie was a winner because he achieved something he could only have dreamed of in his childhood, competing in the Olympic Games. And is that not the Olympic ideal?

Most football clubs can identify one match in their history as being representative of the glorious high point of their existence. Fittingly it seems, for Hartlepool United it was a defeat. However, a 3-4 scoreline against the Busby Babes at their most thrilling was an achievement of which to be proud. The FA Cup third round tie in 1957 would become a part of FA Cup folklore that Matt Busby would later describe in his autobiography as the most exciting match he had ever watched. In fact, Hartlepool specialise in glorious defeat. In 1952 they also lost with honours in the FA Cup third round against First Division high fliers Burnley. The 0-1 defeat was seen by over 38,000 fans at Turf Moor and confirmed their place as one of football's non-winners. They have never survived beyond the fourth round but every time Hartlepool play against a really big club it feels like a victory.

So, for all those who think losing should be avoided at all costs, remember Hartlepool and the immortal words of David Pleat from 1989: "Winning isn't the end of the world."

The 'M' Team

	Seasons	Apps	Goals	Source
Maurice Marston (FB)				
Trimdon, 24 March 1929				
Died 2002				
Sunderland	1949-52	9	0	JNRS
Northampton Town	1953-56	149	2	TR

Interviewed wife January 2001

Born in Trimdon Village, Maurice Marston moved with his family to the Sunderland area as a boy and it was here that he blossomed into a promising young footballer with Redby Juniors and the Bede junior and senior teams. He was signed as a junior by Sunderland after leaving school at fifteen but continued to represent Durham Junior Cup Winners, Silksworth from 1945-47. It was now, aged eighteen that he was called into the army and guested for Rhyl in the Cheshire League. It was clear that he had a future in the game and Sunderland immediately signed him on professional forms after demob' in 1949.

He took part in the club's pioneering trip to Turkey in 1950, one of the first occasions a club had toured The Middle East. However, he had to wait until 15th March 1952 for his League debut against Tottenham Hotspur at White Hart Lane. An attendance of 51,680 saw the twenty-two year old make a solid debut against the team who would finish runners-up behind League Champions Manchester United. Maurice's opposite number that day was none other than Alf Ramsey and the Sunderland team contained Trevor Ford and Len Shackleton. The Football Echo recorded that "...there was no harder fighter in the side than Marston who tackled and recovered well." Maurice's over-riding memory of the day was the support he received from team-mates to help him overcome his nerves. He recalls being handed a bunch of congratulatory telegrams from friends and colleagues on arriving at the ground. Unfortunately the team lost 0-2 but it was a memorable debut.

He would only make eight more League appearances for the 'Bank of England Club' but it was 'an honour' to play with a team so packed with talent. He may have been earning a maximum of £12.50 per week but he felt that the pressure was not as it is today and he's pleased he played when he did. Len Shackleton was a particular friend and colleague with whom he also strapped on the pads for Wearmouth Cricket Club. He was probably the best footballer Maurice was privileged to appear with.

In 1953 he made the switch to Northampton Town in Division Three (South) and regular first team football. Under managers Bob Dennison and Dave Smith he made a total of 149 League appearances in four seasons. 'The Cobblers' were consistently in the top half of the table but never quite managed to make the final push for promotion. Nevertheless, Maurice was a stalwart performer for the club and highly regarded by the fans at The County Ground for his wholehearted approach. In fact the County Ground would have made cricket-loving Maurice quite at home since it was the famous three sided stadium shared by the Northamptonshire County Cricket Club.

In 1957, aged twenty-eight, he decided to quit the professional game while he was still regarded as a good player. He had been studying accountancy for some time in the knowledge that he didn't want to go into management and he needed to prepare for another career. He became an office manager with Earls Barton shoe manufacturing company and continued to play part-time for Kettering Town. He pulled on his boots for the last time in 1965 but five years later returned to Rockingham Road as part-time club secretary when 'The Poppies' were going through a particularly rough time. This was his last formal association with football. Living with his wife, Elizabeth, in Barton Seagrove, Maurice lost his battle with long-term illness in January 2002. Fortunately he had been able to look back on a career in which he enjoyed every minute. In fact, as Elizabeth proudly recalls, it was so good he would have played for nothing.

	Seasons	Apps	Goals	Source
Maurice Mason (IF)				
Sedgefield, 25 June 1927				
Huddersfield Town	1948	0	0	
Darlington	1952	3	0	Blackhall Colliery

Interviewed April 2000

Born a few doors down from the Parish Hall in Sedgefield, Fishburn colliery was Maurice Mason's place of employment after leaving school. He also played a bit of football and was a regular in the Northern League with Ferryhill. In fact, he was good enough to be spotted and signed for £1,000 by First Division Huddersfield in 1948 and remained on a full-time professional contract for two years, playing regularly in the reserve team but never quite making the first eleven in The League. However, he was paid £10 per week for the pleasure as opposed to the £8.50 he picked up at the pit.

When his contract was up he returned to Blackhall Colliery on a full-time contract and stayed there until he was signed by Darlington after a two week trial. He only stayed for a season and a half under managers George Irwin then Bob Gurney. Having only been given three opportunities for the first team in The League he left with his contract paid off in full. Maurice moved back to Ferryhill on a part-time basis and resumed his position at Fishburn, eventually becoming deputy then overman. He stayed until the pit closed and moved on to brick laying.

His football effectively ended aged 27 with ankle and knee injuries and ten shillings insurance money. Nowadays he watches his football on TV and confesses he misses playing. But he had a good time, particularly at Leeds Road and is proud of the recognition and respect he gained from local people at Huddersfield.

	Seasons	Apps	Goals	Source
Walter Miller (WH)				
Cornforth, 11 August 1930				
Hartlepool Utd	1949	3	0	
Luton Town	1952	0	0	Spennymoor Utd

Cornforth born Walter Miller played his three League matches under the legendary Fred Westgarth at The Victoria Ground. Unfortunately, the coming together of Newton, Stamper and Moore on the half-back line meant his chances were restricted and he was released in 1950. After a spell at Spennymoor United in the Northern League he was picked up by Second Division Luton Town. In his one season at Kenilworth Road, the club almost made it to the top division, finishing a creditable third behind Sheffield United and Huddersfield Town. However, Walter never made the first eleven and was released by manager Dally Duncan in 1953.

	Seasons	Apps	Goals	Source
Thomas Moore (G) Trimdon, 25 July 1936 Darlington (Am)	1956	1	0	Winterton

Interviewed August 2001

Tommy Moore had been an outstanding schoolboy goalkeeper representing Durham County on a number of occasions, one of which, against Lancashire when his opposite number was Eddie Hopkinson who went on to star for Bolton and England. After leaving school at fifteen, he was taken on as an apprentice painter and decorator at Winterton hospital where he also played football and cricket. Whilst at Winterton he was encouraged by Darlington manager, Bob Gurney, to sign as an amateur at Feethams where he played many reserve team matches in the four years leading up to his one and only League appearance in 1956. However, Darlington was not his first club. Huddersfield Town had courted him as a junior and he had spent some time at Leeds Road playing in the Intermediate League before returning back home.

During his period as a Darlington reserve he was kept out of the first eleven by Billy Dunn, Don Cowans and Tom Clish. However, he had a forced eight-month absence from the game in 1955 after suffering a serious medial ligament injury against West Stanley. Doctors advised him that he may not play again and in truth, he was probably never the same after that set back. Nevertheless, on the 13th April 1956 he was elevated to the first team for his solitary League appearance at home to York City. They lost 2-4 against one of York's best ever teams that had reached the semi-final of the FA Cup in the previous season. Tommy, by his own admission, had a poor game against a team including the opponent he most admired, centre forward Arthur Bottom. His knee injury was a constant concern by now and not only had he played his last game for Darlington but he barely kicked another ball again, even refusing the opportunity to return to Winterton.

Tommy Moore (the tall one at the back) for Trimdon in 1955. (Photo: Sunderland Echo)

He enjoyed his association with The Quakers though and had a particular admiration for chairman, John Neasham who was a genuine supporter of the club. He also recalls the times Manchester United's Eddie Colman joined the team on Tommy's twice-a-week training sessions. On national service and based at Catterick, Feethams was a convenient venue for Colman to practice with professionals as his career prepared to take off. Sadly, he was to perish at Munich in 1958 still aged only twenty-two.

Tommy also fondly remembers trainer Dickie Deacon who would soak the leather case balls in a bath of water if he felt the opponents were a little light-weight. The heavier the ball, the better. And finally, there was the Footballing Father, John Caden who was on the Darlington books in 1952 and allegedly even appeared for the club under a false name. Certainly, on one occasion he kept goal legitimately for Darlington RA in a match against Darlington reserves for whom Tommy was doing the same job. Father Caden still administers the sacraments in Sedgefield to this day.

As far as his career goes, Tommy sometimes wishes he'd joined the police force when he was younger and he certainly wishes he'd taken his City and Guilds exams more seriously instead of playing football and going to the pictures. The knees have plagued him in later life and are now both artificial joints. He is also learning to live, at home in Trimdon Grange, with the effects of a stroke in 1996. But whilst dogged by ill-health, he has the joy of his grand children to lift his spirits and the knowledge that he was one of the few people good enough to step across the touch-line into the Football League.

is for Minister

On 22nd June 1995 John Major resigned as leader of the Tory Party. He felt he had taken his team as far as he could in the circumstances, the circumstances being that they were split down the middle on a number of issues, most notably European policy. Three days later on 25th of June Kenny Dalglish resigned as manager of Blackburn Rovers. Tired and stressed, he felt he had taken his team as far as he could under the circumstances.

On 26th of June John Redwood challenged John Major for leadership of the Tory Party and on the same day Ray Harford replaced Kenny Dalglish as manager of Blackburn Rovers. Both men were in like a rat up a drainpipe as their predecessors apparently buckled under the pressure of the responsibilities of office. Redwood was a disaster as a potential leader and Harford a disaster as a manager, both failing to realise their chosen ambition. The similarities between football management and political leadership are striking. They carry similar burdens with the expectations of a large following, the pressure to meet promises made before taking the reins, the need to mould a team from a group of disparate talents and the feeling of isolation when things are not going to plan.

The one big difference between managers and politicians is that politicians often associate themselves with football clubs but rarely does a football manager 'come out' as a political animal. Notable exceptions to the latter are Alex Ferguson and Brian Clough who both declared themselves staunch Labour. It would be interesting to take some of our famous managers and MP's and test the similarity theory by having them change places. After all, it was Harold Wilson no less, who declared,

"I know more about football than politics."

How about Gordon Brown for Arsenal. The famously 'prudent' Chancellor would find the rigid wage structure at Highbury most agreeable and being pro-European would be at home amongst all the foreigners. Arsene Wenger would make an ideal pro-European Chancellor being one himself and has a speaking style equally as boring as Brown's. In fact these two are totally inter-changeable. William Hague could have done a job-swap with Jim Smith at Derby County. Some have commented on the flat-vowelled, gritty, northern realism that Hague brought to the despatch box. Just think how much flatter the vowels, how much more gritty, more northern and more realistic politics would have been with Jim Smith on the front bench. On the other hand, William Hague would have been at home with his baseball cap on the sidelines and when he removed it, would anyone have noticed that he's not Jim Smith.

Finally, there's Paddy Ashdown. He could have managed England and Fulham. One in need of military-style intervention and the other a team whose best days were years ago but are scenting recovery and a whiff of success. Kevin Keegan would have replaced Paddy as leader of the Liberal Democrats, becoming everyone's favourite politician and taking the Liberals to the brink of power. Unfortunately, Labour leader, Alex Ferguson would psyche him out just as he looks like becoming PM and Keegan would be seen screaming across the floor of the House, "I'll love it if we beat you at the next election. Just love it."

The 'N' Team

	Seasons	Apps	Goals	Source
Irving Nattrass (RB)				
Fishburn, 12 December 1952	Eu23-1			
Newcastle Utd	1970-78	238	16	APP
Middlesbrough	1979-85	191	2	TR

Interviewed February 2000

Irving Nattrass played his entire career on the banks of the Tyne and the Tees. Despite numerous opportunities to move elsewhere, most notably Everton, Arsenal and Leeds, his natural affinity with the North-East kept him in the area. It was a career that he modestly believes may not have begun at all had it not been for the fact that Newcastle United had not taken their maximum quota for the 12-14 year age band of schoolboys in 1967. Local scout Harry Nattrass (no relation) recommended him and he was given his first opportunity at fourteen. His association with the club lasted from 1967-1978, his League debut coming in the First Division 0-2 defeat at Coventry City in 1971 in the last game of the season. He had been an apprentice at St. James Park when, in 1969, The Magpies won the European Fairs Cup. It was a magical time to be around the club even for the apprentices who were painting the turnstiles, sweeping the terraces and cleaning the star boots. And the stars themselves? - Well they didn't act like stars. They treated everyone at the club with respect and Newcastle was a happy place to be. Perhaps the main reason for this was manager Joe Harvey, whom Irving describes as a 'great man' with a 'fantastic presence'. He was a man-manager and motivator who never felt the need to shout at his charges. He had a strangely calming voice. Another significant authority at the club was coach, Keith Birkinshaw who did most of the hands-on work with the players and was perhaps the greatest influence on Irving's career.

1969-1977 was one of the most successful in Newcastle's history. The Fairs Cup triumph was followed by victory in the Anglo-Italian Cup in 1973, an FA Cup Final appearance in 1974, a League Cup Final appearance in 1975 and further qualification for the UEFA Cup in 1977-78, the season they were also to be relegated to The Second Division. Irving Nattrass, the boy from Fishburn, was there throughout. His personal highlight was the 1-2 League Cup Final defeat against Manchester City. It was a good contest and an entertaining game unlike the 1974 FA Cup Final that had seen Newcastle humiliated by a rampant Liverpool. Irving missed that game recovering from a knee injury. Another highlight was appearing in the UEFA Cup in 1977-78. Unfortunately, it only lasted until the second round when they were eliminated by the eventual beaten finalists, Bastia.

Many people would assume that the low point of his career came in 1972. Irving Nattrass was one of the Newcastle team that drew 2-2 at home to non-league Hereford before sensationally losing 1-2 in the replay at Edgar Street in what was the greatest FA Cup shock in history. However, he says that the feeling was one of numbness rather than disappointment. No-one spoke afterwards in the changing room or on the bus. They simply couldn't believe what had happened to them. What people forget though, is that Newcastle followed this humbling experience with a 2-0 victory at Old Trafford in front of 60,000 fans against opposition boasting Best, Law and Charlton. The result cured the FA Cup hangover in a flash. The true low points for Irving were the 1972 mediate ligament injury that kept him out of the game for six months and relegation from the First Division in 1978. The manager was Bill McGarry, ex Wolves and a man with a hard reputation, which he set about proving to everyone he met at the club. McGarry ruled by fear, including the schoolboys and apprentices and according to Irving Nattrass, could be nasty and vindictive. The result was a loss of support, loss of morale and inevitable relegation. Irving left the club at the first opportunity, which happened to be a transfer to Middlesbrough for a then club record fee of £475,000.

It was a big fee and it sent Irving straight back into the First Division with an exciting Boro side that included Procter, Johnston, Hodgson and Armstrong. He regards this as possibly the best team he appeared in, certainly equal to the 1975 Newcastle team but unfortunately, as is often the case at Middlesbrough, a team reached the point of greatness and turned back as if afraid to make that last step to the highest level. Once again, Boro got a nosebleed and began a free fall that saw them in Division Three in 1986. Irving had been a particular fan of John Neal whom he placed in the same category as a manager and a man as Joe Harvey.

In 1985 he was faced with a major decision in light of the new manager, Bruce Rioch's plans to introduce young blood. Should he attempt to continue his professional career or call it a day and concentrate on developing the clothing retail business he had started? He chose the latter knowing that he was leaving the game in good health and on his own terms. In fact, that business still provides his living with six branches of the 'Chainstore Clothing Co.' in and around the Newcastle area. Rioch was a hard man in the McGarry mould but without the vindictive streak. Irving had respect for him and his achievements but did wonder whether or not he could sustain success in one place because of his rather inflexible disciplinarian methods. Looking back, our discussion reminds him of his one regret, that he didn't give management a try.

Indeed, managers featured heavily in our conversation. His respect for Harvey and Neal and his disdain for the McGarry style. His sadness at the way in which Alf Ramsey, 'a great gentleman, a nice man and way ahead of his time', was so shabbily treated by the FA. His excitement at the impact the 'great Bobby Robson' is having on his beloved Newcastle and the inappropriateness of Ruud Gullit. His liking for Gordon Lee, 'a good manager whose big mistake was to sell 'SuperMac' and his regret that Bryan Robson ran out of steam at the Boro. Perhaps he should have tried management after all.

However, he can look back with pride on an almost continuous First Division career, a Wembley Cup Final appearance, an under 23 international cap for England and inclusion in the full squad for the Hungary friendly in 1975. If it were not for David Nish and Paul Reaney, the international tally could have been much greater. He had the honour of facing Pele in an end of season tour with Newcastle when the team took on Santos in Hong Kong. Pele scored a hat-trick; 'he leapt as if he had springs on his feet'. During the 2-4 defeat, Tony Green scored a brilliant 30-yard scorcher. Green was perhaps the best player Irving shared a team-sheet with; a giant talent whose career was cut short by a poor diagnosis of a cartilage injury.

The Nattrass family now lives happily near Ashington. Irving doesn't play football any more. In fact apart from a brief spell with Evenwood years ago he effectively left the game when he left Middlesbrough. He still follows his old teams though and occasionally gets to a game and it's interesting to note that when he talks about 'us' he is talking about Newcastle. That's where his football heart truly belongs.

	Seasons	Apps	Goals	Source
Keith Nobbs (RB)				
Bishop Middleham, 18 September 1961				
Middlesbrough	1980-82	1	0	APP
Halifax Town	1982-83	87	1	TR
Hartlepool United	1985-92	280	6	Bishop Auckland

Interviewed February 2000

Most of the record books show that Keith Nobbs was born in Bishop Auckland but he is actually Bishop Middleham through and through and like many of the up and coming pro's from the area in the eighties, he got his first break with Middlesbrough.

His thirteen-year career as a professional culminated in eight years of solid, dependable service at right-back for Hartlepool with one of the better Pools teams since the war. His time at the club coincided with that of Tinkler, Honour, McKinnon and Baker amongst others and was suitably rewarded by promotion to the Third Division in 1990/91 and a further two seasons in that league with creditable mid-table finishes. He also shared in the 0-5 League Cup defeat at Tottenham Hotspur that featured a rampant, Lazio-bound Paul Gascoigne who scored four goals. This was the best opponent he ever faced, a genius at the height of his powers.

However, the Hartlepool years were not universally successful or easy to navigate. He had arrived there from a one-year sabbatical in the Northern League at Bishop Auckland when Billy Horner, who had stayed in touch with Keith, invited him to the Victoria Ground. The club was struggling and many players were on year to year contracts. Bob Newton was also re-signed for his second spell at the club and Alan Shoulder joined the team from Carlisle. The club continued to hint at success and promotion for the next few seasons under Horner, John Bird and Bob Moncur but it was the Cyril Knowles and Alan Murray years from 1989 that saw this Hartlepool team realise it's potential. Mind you, they tried everything they could, Bird even enlisting the talents of ex-miner and British rock 'n' roll champion, 70-year-old Lennie Hepple, the guru of rhythm and movement. He was charged with improving the movement, co-ordination and balance of the players, something he'd previously achieved with World Cup Captain, Bobby Moore. Well, if it's good enough for him.... Keith's time at the Victoria Ground was characterised by commitment, effort and reliability, features which can't be instilled by a dance teacher but nevertheless, made him a favourite with the fans.

He had begun his career in 1977 as an apprentice at Ayresome Park under Jack Charlton, being trained by the diminutive George Wardle in the carpark at the back of the ground. Many-a-time the ball would have to be retrieved from the grounds of Middlesbrough General next door. But it was George who fired Keith's enthusiasm for the pro game. These were good times at Boro when the likes of Craig Johnston, David Hodgson and Mark Procter were breaking through and older pros like John Craggs were guiding the young guns. Keith remembers Johnston as 'tremendously skillful and a great athlete', possibly the best he's played with. He also remembers transporting young hopefuls, Colin Cooper and Paul Ward to training from Trimdon. However, League appearances for Keith Nobbs were to be restricted to just one outing at home to Coventry City in 1981. He can barely recall the game; it just flashed by. But he knows he enjoyed it and that is the most important thing to him.

The move to the Shay Ground, Halifax, was the guarantee of first team football that Keith needed. He spent two full seasons at the Fourth Division club under Micky Bullock, himself a former Halifax player. There was not too much by way of atmosphere in the ground, as he recalls. It was very open and while the playing surface was good, it was surrounded by the speedway track, further distancing the players from the sparse crowds. Indeed the speedway meetings regularly attracted 8,000 spectators, well above the average for football matches. He enjoyed Halifax but the set-up was very basic compared to Middlesbrough. Training was generally very physical with far less emphasis ball work than the methods of Middlesbrough coaches Murdoch and Wardle. This tended to reflect the difference between the two Leagues as well. Budgetary problems at The Shay forced Keith to opt for a move to Bishop Auckland rather than risk short term contracts on poor money. The move proved temporary as the watchful Billy Horner monitored his form and eventually took him to Hartlepool.

After eight good years at The Victoria Ground he left for Gateshead where he played part-time for three years. Hartlepool's promotion seasons had left them with a high wage bill and financial problems, something familiar to most small clubs. However, he was to return again, to his present employment as Football in the Community Officer at United. Mick Tait, manager in 1998 informed him of the opportunity and Keith began accumulating coaching qualifications. He's currently studying for his UEFA 'B' badge (the one David Platt should have had at Sampdoria) and is doing great work in schools.

He's currently looking for a plot of land to build a new home, possibly at Hamsterly and he's enjoying his continued involvement in the game he loves. Keith Nobbs is a man with no regrets from his career. It was just great to earn a living playing football.

N is for Nationality

The end of the 20th century saw more genuine discussion and debate about nationality than at any other time in modern history. Suddenly, everyone was obsessed by identity and many were troubled by doubts about which national family they actually belonged to. Am I English, British or European? Am I Catalonian or Spanish? Serbian or Yugoslavian? Who exactly do I identify with? These and other questions have lead to tensions across the globe and a world ill at ease with itself aat the turn of the millennium.

Modern, professional sport adds a further dimension to this soul searching. What nationality would be best for my career? Consider the following international performers: English cricketer Alan Lamb, Scottish footballer Don Hutchison, Welsh footballer Vinnie Jones, British tennis star Greg Rusedski, Irish footballer Ray Houghton, Italian athlete Fiona May. They're all great at what they do but probably couldn't even hum their national anthem let alone sing the words.

It is arguable that this blurring of national identity can only be a good thing since it helps to break down the barriers between different cultures and develop a greater understanding of one another. The trouble is that it becomes more difficult to use our national stereotypes to assess players. It used to be so easy. The Argentinians were hackers. The Italians were cheats. The French were all 'Gallic flair'. The Africans were naïve. The Spanish were chokers. The Scandinavians were emerging. We could talk about Latin temperament, German efficiency and the Slavs being 'happy on the ball'. We could patronise the Americans and the Australians and marvel at how small the 'big man up front' was in the Japanese team.

Now we have efficient Brazilians, temperamental Germans, tall Japanese and Scandinavians who are 'happy on the ball'. Thank God the Spanish are still chokers and we can still patronise the Australians.

To play for one's country must be the most chest-plumpingly proud, yet humbling experience. To play for someone else's must be an interesting test of your own loyalty and integrity. At the same time, we as the spectators, supporters and financers of sport want to see the best performers at the highest level, against the best opposition, pushing back the boundaries of human achievement and thrilling us in a way that only sport can. And football is the most thrilling of all sports. Witness the Manchester United v Bayern Munich European Champions Cup final on May 26th 1999. Two multi-national teams where once they would be almost exclusively English and German, but has sport ever produced such theatre, such raw emotion?

And for once the English won - with a goal by a Norwegian.

The 'O' Team

	Seasons	Apps	Goals	Source
Thomas O'Neill (RB)				
Spennymoor, 5 January 1925 Died 1978				
Newcastle Utd	1942	0	0	Spennymoor Utd
Newport County	1948	9	0	TR

As a seventeen-year-old, Tom O'Neill was a full-back in the Spennymoor team of the early war years. His talents were recognised by Second Division Newcastle United, managed by Stan Seymour and he was taken to St. James' Park but never made a League appearance. As the war continued his professional career, like many others, was rudely interrupted. Though during 1943 and 1944 he turned out for Leeds United as The League was suspended and many players called up to the forces appeared for clubs close to where they were stationed. After the final whistle was blown on Hiltler, Tom returned to The League with Newcastle without success and eventually moved on to Newport County and manager Tom Bromilow. He appeared nine times in League games for 'The Ironsides', his debut coming in the first game of the 1948-49 season, a 1-2 defeat at Bournemouth. His final appearance came in a 2-5 defeat at Orient, his career coming to an abrupt end after breaking a leg in a subsequent reserve match at Somerton Park in March 1949. After receiving a free transfer he returned briefly to play for Spennymoor but soon turned around and settled back in Wales where he spent the rest of his days before dying in Newport in 1978. Ten years later Newport would be relegated from The League never to return.

	Seasons	Apps	Goals	Source
Eric Oliver (G)				
Spennymoor, 8 July 1940				
Darlington (Am)	1963	2	0	West Auckland

Eric Oliver was one of four goalkeepers used by Darlington manager, Eddie Carr in the 1963/64 season. Signed on amateur forms whilst playing for West Auckland in the Northern League, he was cover for Chris Penman who had taken over mid-season from Keith Hird. His two appearances came in February 1964 in a 1-1 home draw with Gillingham and the next fixture, a 1-3 away defeat at Southport. The team went on to finish 19th in Division Four by which time Irish international Jimmy O'Neill had been signed from Stoke City and Eric, who was no longer required, returned to the non-league scene.

	Seasons	Apps	Goals	Source
George Outhwaite (G)				
Ferryhill, 19 May 1928				
Oldham Athletic (Am)	1955	4	0	Chilton Colliery

Interviewed August 2001

Most of George's career was spent at Bishop Auckland, Spennymoor and Durham City where he was courted variously by Manchester Utd and Bradford City for whom he could have signed professional forms. He was a member of the Bishop's side that reached the semi-final of the Amateur Cup and included Bobby Hardisty and he was a Durham player when they made their first ever appearance at Ferrens Park. His was a distinguished amateur career. George was famous for his penalty saves, once stopping nine in a row. He was also famous for his diminutive stature as a goalkeeper, a fact that was trotted out in almost every newspaper article that mentioned him. He even found himself forced onto the 'George Walsh Body-Bulk' plan to build him up, some people even hoping it might make him taller. However, he got his call-up to The League in 1956 when Oldham Athletic had just transferred one 'keeper to Sunderland and had another on the treatment table. The Latics' coach, Trimdon's own football guru, Owen Willoughby, knew of George as a gifted non-league performer and had no hesitation in having him taxied up to Redheugh Park, Gateshead. Aged twenty-seven years and 302 days he made his League debut in a 3-1 victory, predictably saving a penalty along the way. After the match, the team coach dropped him off on the old A1 outside Ferryhill on its way back to Lancashire. George walked the rest of the way home. Co-incidentally, two other local lads, George Crook (Easington born) and Kenny Chaytor played for Oldham that day. He also recalls a couple of other occasions when he was collected from Rochdale train station by manager, George Hardwick who then personally took him to the Oldham lodgings where he would stay for the weekend.

George Outhwaite demonstrates his legendary springy legs for Durham City in 1955

Like many in his position, however, he preferred to work full-time and play part-time. He spent thirty-three years at Thorns in Spennymoor, finally taking early retirement at the age of fifty-nine when Electrolux took over. Luckily, the company pension scheme was good enough to allow him to indulge in his new pastimes, golf, bowls and holidays. And as far as his football career is concerned, George reckons that at five feet seven inches he may have been too short to make it in goal although he was known for his exceptional agility. As he says, "I never quite made it but I had a great time."

is for Opinions

"Football's all about opinions."

God, how I hate that expression. But like most cliches it is at least founded in truth if not entirely correct. Arguing the finer points of a match after the event is part and parcel of the national game whether it be in the pub, in the newspapers, at work the next day or on one of the proliferation of radio phone-in shows 'where the fans have their say'. However, it is not the fans but the managers who, more than anyone, have their contrasting views so nakedly aired at the end of each game in the post-match interview. Television has truly taken the clash of opinion to new dimensions. It is instant, spontaneous and conducted while the sweat is still fresh on the brow. It therefore can occasionally be highly combustible - great TV.

Victorious manager: "To be fair, I thought the ref did well today. It was never going to be easy."

Defeated manager: "That was the worst refereeing performance I've seen this season. He's given them a penalty when their boy has taken a dive and he's turned down a certain penalty for us when their lad has blatantly handled the ball. All we want is consistency - that's the fourth time this year the ref has cost us the points. To be fair - he's had a stinker and he hasn't even had the guts to admit his mistake.....Anyway, I don't want to say anything about the referee."

However, the TV spotlight has forced many interviewees to adopt new tactics. Top-flight managers have now perfected the art of the non-opinion to get their views across.

The issue of penalties or serious sending-off incidents usually brings this particular arrow out of the managerial quiver.

Sinned against manager: "That was a diabolical tackle. The lad's gone in with two feet and taken him out by the groin. He'll be disappointed with himself when he's sees that on video."

Manager of sinner: "I noticed there was a bit of a clash but I couldn't see it properly from the dug-out. It was a good, physical game."

Of course, the gaffer is also capable of expressing views on contemporary issues within a socio-political context bringing to bear all his experience of human resource management and appreciation of the limitless potential of humankind. Take Ron Atkinson for instance, speaking on BBC 2 in 1989:

"Women should be in the kitchen, the discotheque and the boutique, but not in football."

Well, it's an opinion.

The 'P' Team

	Seasons	Apps	Goals	Source
John Parkinson (WH) Trimdon, 2 June 1953 Hartlepool Utd (Am)	1971	1	0	Trimdon Jnrs

Interviewed September 2001

When John Parkinson eventually made his League debut with Hartlepool versus Newport County, the die was probably already cast for his career in football. After playing a few reserve games, he was thrown in as an amateur and performed creditably in midfield. Well enough in fact to be invited back to play on Boxing Day. He didn't turn up. He rang in with an excuse but manager Len Ashurst was having none of it. He wasn't invited again and frankly, John wasn't too bothered.

As a promising talent with Trimdon Juniors, John had been spotted by Derby County scouts when their junior team had a fixture arranged against the village team. He had impressed enough to be invited to The Baseball Ground and spent a month with Cloughie's emerging squad. He was even shown the place he would live when he signed and had the dubious honour of being told by Brian Clough to get his hair cut. Unfortunately, a breach of discipline - attending a nightclub - was followed by a last chance ultimatum for him to shine in a trial match. To his dismay, he was asked to play full-back and did not perform. He was on his way home. This rejection by Derby lead to disillusionment and when his chance came at Hartlepool, the motivation had all but evaporated. John didn't play again until he took up local league football in his mid to late twenties. He admits to looking back occasionally and wondering what might have been.

However, the years weren't wasted. He had attended Hartlepool tech' after leaving school and his joinery apprenticeship proved to be the basis of his future livelihood. He is now a partner in a joinery business and has recently built his own home in Cassop. The arthritic knees won't allow football now - it's firmly in the past.

	Seasons	Apps	Goals	Source
Norman Parsley (WH) Shildon, 28 November 1923. Died 1993 Darlington	1946-52	161	14	Shildon Wks

Interviewed widow May 1999

Wilf Parsley, as he was known, had a seven-year career as a league footballer but never turned full-time, preferring instead to remain in his job at the Shildon Works while there was still some life left in the railways. Born in Shildon but brought up in Leeholme, he was a schoolboy trialist with Manchester Utd and played at Ferryhill and Shildon before being taken to Feethams by manager, Bill Forrest. Perhaps marrying young pursuaded him to opt for the part-time route since he could top-up his Works pay packet with £5 per week from his football with the promise of a £2 win bonus on a good day. Wife, Freda would sit and watch the games with the players' wives and thoroughly enjoyed following the team's progress.

Wilf Parsley poses in his Darlington strip in 1949. You could've ironed his shirt Freda.

His career was effectively ended by a bad tackle that left him with a plate and screw in an ankle. However, though he derived a great deal of satisfaction from playing the game, he was not a good spectator and became somewhat disillusioned with football after leaving Darlington. He preferred cricket and played for Coundon for many years before illness took a hold.

	Seasons	Apps	Goals	Source
Michael Peacock (G)				
Fishburn, 28 September 1940				
Darlington	1960-62	46	0	Shildon

Interviewed July 1999

Throughout Mike Peacock's short career he continued working at Fishburn Colliery, his £7 per week from Darlington supplementing his electrician's wage during the football season. In fact, he blames his part-time status for his eventual divorce from Darlington. He found himself training at different times from many of his full-time colleagues and when Jim Ferguson was brought in from Crewe Alexander, Mike feels that a certain amount of pressure was placed on manager, Eddie Carr by the full-timers, to have the new 'keeper in the team. Consequently, at the end of the 1962-63 season, Mike left the club to join the prison service. He saw little future in the pits and no future for himself in football. He'd had approaches by Liverpool, West Ham and Leicester City but decided his future lay elsewhere. He went on to appear for the prison service and for Knaresborough before becoming a class one referee.

He had originally been spotted playing for Trimdon Grange in the Wearside League and later, Shildon in the Northern League. Eddie Carr snapped him up in August 1960 and he soon made his debut, aged 19 yrs, in a 2-2 draw at home to Peterborough in the Fourth Division. He went on to play with the likes of Malcolm Dawes, Ron Greener, George Mulholland and Ken Furphy but remembers Lance Robson as a potentially great talent. Lance was known to his club-mates as 'The Mad Dentist' because of his slightly out-of-control antics and the fact that he was actually fully qualified in the teeth business. The opponent Mike most admired was Ernie Hunt of Swindon who starred in a 4-0 defeat of Darlington in the League Cup second round in 1962. This was the man who became famous for the outrageous 'flipped-up-and-volleyed' free kick that used to appear on the opening credits of Match of The day.

Nowadays, he watches the progress of Darlington with interest since the club was bought by millionaire businessman, George Reynolds. He hopes the new man proves to be as dedicated a benefactor as John Neasham who personally installed the first floodlights at Feethams in 1961. Indeed, the mention of floodlights brings back memories of playing at Doncaster Rovers where the Belle Vue Ground had such utterly hopeless lights that you couldn't see the players from certain positions, one of which was in goal. The game also featured soon-to-be comedian, Charlie Williams of Golden Shot fame.

Based in Northallerton, Mike is now retired, busy playing bowls and tending the local cricket pitch.

	Seasons	Apps	Goals	Source
John Pearson (IF) Ferryhill, 8 May 1951 Hartlepool Utd (Am)	1968	1	0	Ferryhill Athletic

Interviewed November 1999

Put yourself in John Pearson's boots. You've been spotted scoring goals for fun at Ferryhill and the manager of Hartlepool, in this case Gus McClean, offers you the opportunity to try your hand at League football. You sign as an amateur and play in a Third Division fixture at Stockport. The only problem is that you get paid £3 and it costs you £4 in bus fares and other expenses to join up with the team bus. When you mention to the manager that this seems a little perverse, he observes that you're only an amateur, what do you expect? You may feel inclined to think that someone is taking you for a ride. John Pearson did and decided to put up two metaphorical fingers to Hartlepool. And so a Football League career came and went.

It was followed by a short spell at Coventry City where John played a number of reserve games during the reign of manager, Jimmy Hill, but he never settled there. Hill was a hard taskmaster and the full-time pros formed unwelcoming cliques. It was a difficult time for the Ferryhill home bird and he duly returned to the North where he spent a number of happy and successful seasons playing for Ferryhill, Crook, Willington and South Shields often topping his team's goal-scoring charts. Cruelly, a cruciate ligament injury effectively ended his playing career at the age of 24 and deprived him of travelling with Crook Town on the famous India tour in 1976. His brother, David replaced him on the trip-of-a-lifetime and once again John was left to rue his misfortune. However, there were highlights, in particular appearing for Willington against Blackburn Rovers in the FA Cup 3rd round, drawing 0-0 at home then losing 0-7 in the replay at Ewood Park before 9,000 fans.

He had served his time as a toolmaker and eventually became a manufacturing supervisor in the engineering industry. But football is in the veins (and in the family, brother Mattie is manager of Gateshead as we speak) and he still manages the Ferryhill Greyhound over 40's. Although he regrets his lack of ambition and application as far as pro' football is concerned, he still loves the game more than anything... "If it could cook I would marry it."

	Seasons	Apps	Goals	Source
Raymond Pennick (IF) Ferryhill, 30 Nov 1946 York City (Am)	1968	1	0	Willlington

Interviewed June 1999

Ray Pennick had been a top performer in the Northern League with Ferryhill, Willington and Spennymoor before completing his teacher training qualification in 1967 at Sheffield. It was whilst in his first year as a PE teacher at Spennymoor Grammar School, he turned out for Willington against York City reserves and the League club were so impressed they put immediate pressure on him to sign for them. He succumbed and somewhat reluctantly signed amateur forms appearing in one game, a floodlit 0-0 draw with Halifax in which he played for the final 30 minutes alongside Ted MacDougal and Ian Bowyer. However, the match will always be remembered by those who were present for the sudden collapse and death of referee, Roy Harper, after 8 minutes. The game was understandably delayed for some time but after a respectful period of inaction, resumed with the linesman, Bill Johnson, taking the whistle and as Ray put it, "some old bloke in an overcoat from the stand running the line."

As coincidence would have it, a 13 year old Halifax fan watching the game with his father, also decided to become a teacher and eventually gained his first full time post in the same school as Ray. Steve Tose had never forgotten the match or the name Pennick and recounts the 'Halifax story' at every opportunity. In fact, at a staff Fantasy Football League presentation evening on 18th June 1999, Ray was presented with a letter from York City and the relevant page from a book about former City players relating his story. Three days later a complete stranger, writing a book about footballers from the Sedgefield area, contacted him to talk about his game in The Football League. Spooky eh?

It looks like Ray, now teaching at Hetton School, will dine out on this story for years. It may have been a short career but it wasn't boring.

	Seasons	Apps	Goals	Source
Joseph Porteous (LH) Shildon, 20 April 1925 York City	1946	23	0	Chesterfield (Am)

Shildon born Joe was one of the thirty-four players used by York in the first season of League football following the resumption of normal activities after the war. Many players were still required for National Service so large squads were not unusual. He had been an amateur half-back with Chesterfield during the war years but was picked up by manager Tom Mitchell after trials in August 1946. A series of good displays in the reserves lead to an extended run in the first team, his debut coming in a 1-3 defeat by Wrexham on 26th October in the Third Division (North). It wasn't to be a long-term relationship with Bootham Crescent, however, with Joe moving to Goole Town in 1948 and settling into Midland League football.

is for Preston

Preston-North-End.

There, I've said it. Not Preston United or Preston City or Preston Rovers. Not Preston Town or Preston Wanderers or even Preston Athletic. No, it's Preston-North-End, a name that oozes gritty, northern practicality and which has intrigued me ever since I first heard it. It just sounds like a proper football club.

The very name inspires images of flat caps and rattles; of long shorts and Pathe news; of working-class hordes on post-war open terraces. Those were the days when you actually had to go to a ground to watch a game; when Sky was where the rain came from and television was a new-fangled box in the corner. This was the Golden Era when Tom Finney, 'the Preston Plumber' was the toast of the nation, a one-club, seventy-six cap, home-bred hero whom Bill Shankly famously claimed "would have been great in any team, in any match and in any age.....even if he'd been wearing an overcoat."

Deepdale has seen continuous football since 1879 when it was still home to the North End cricket and rugby clubs. They gave the summer game and the oval ball the boot in 1881 and Preston became a football club. One of twelve founder members of the Football League, they were the first champions in 1888-89 when they also won the FA Cup and they defended the championship the following year. Their last major trophy was the 1938 FA Cup win against Huddersfield Town, though they were once beaten finalists and twice championship runners-up in the 1950's. Since then, they've been up

and down the League, recently more down than up but now they're knocking on the door of the top division for the first time since 1970. This is a club that drips with the history of the game. So much so in fact that Deepdale is now home to the country's National Football Museum

Of course, I will always be grateful to North End for being the source of my 1973 Cup Final ticket. Due to a fortuitous family connection at the club we secured a couple of tickets to the Leeds end of the ground only to find that most of the people were Sunderland fans. I was able to view one of the greatest Cup Final upsets in history only by perching my thirteen-year-old frame on a coke tin such was the density of the crowd. Memories of the play are therefore patchy since I probably missed a good deal of it. However, I will always remember the trophy glinting in the sun as Bobby Kerr hoisted it in triumph to the accompaniment of an ear-splitting roar. It seemed as if the cup itself had thrown out a sunbeam in glorious celebration like a theatre spot-light turning on the crowd to pick out the laughing faces of the audience.

And I will never forget that it was all because of Preston North End.

there are many forms
of communication,
choose the right one...

is for Queue

The 'Q' Team

There is no League player from the Sedgefield area whose name begins with Q. There is of course one who resides here and is a living Irish legend, Niall Quinn. However, if you're looking for daft names, how about Patrick Quartermain who played for Oxford in the 1960's.

So we all agree, football has changed. It's lost much of the romance and innocence of days gone by, overtaken by commercial responsibility and vested interests. But there is one thing that is fast disappearing from the modern game that no-one will miss, the queue.

Take a typical match from the 60's or 70's. You are desperate to support the lads in the forthcoming big match so you queue up for three hours in the pouring rain to get a ticket.

On match day itself you go for a pint before the game and queue to get served at the bar because everyone has decided to do the same, such is the excitement in anticipation of the main event. You get somewhere near to the ground and find yourself squeezed along the road by the liquid rush of fans funneling into the back streets behind the stadium towards the neck of the funnel, which is the turnstile. This is the worst kind of queue because you're not in control and you can't see your feet.

Once through the gate and into the brief respite on the inside of the ground, you queue for a programme - only a short queue but a queue nevertheless. It's now time for the toilet to empty the bladder for the start of the game. You queue for the urinals in the knowledge that when you get in there you will be paddling in piss and anxious to avoid being 'splashed'. When you're relieved, you shove your way onto the terrace - in front of a barrier if possible to avoid being crushed by the surge of the crowd - then observe the game from the comfort of a concrete step with a strange yellow river trickling down it. At half-time you queue for a

Bovril and a burger - Oscar Wilde famously described huntsmen as 'the unspeakable in pursuit of the uneatable', a phrase that could equally have been applied to Millwall fans queuing for their interval refreshments. Then when the match is over you queue to get out and carry defeat on sunken shoulders in an ebb-tide of fans retreating to the town centre where you queue for a bus to go home.

Now, I recently attended Middlesbrough v Bolton at the Riverside Stadium. I had popped to the ground on the way home from work, parked the car outside the ticket office and picked up the tickets I had ordered and paid for over the telephone. Having also been given a parking ticket, on match day I parked within twenty yards of the stadium, had a browse around the old dock, walked straight into the stadium and up to the top of the west stand. We fancied a pint so turned immediately to the bar where we received instant service and supped a comfortable pint amid convivial conversation. Ten minutes before kick-off we took our seats, having purchased a programme from an eager salesperson. We then proceeded to watch forty-five minutes of not-bad football before getting a Bovril and a packet of crisps in an instant and walking straight to a urinal to evacuate the bladder without a single shred of concern for the Hush Puppies.

The second half was dreadful but when the whistle blew we were able to leave the stadium in a flash and be back at the car in less than a minute. We then sat in a traffic jam for fifty minutes just to get out of the car-park. Well, you can't have everything, can you?

The 'R' 'Team

	Seasons	Apps	Goals	Source
Frederick Richardson (CF)				
Spennymoor, 18 August 1925				
Chelsea	1946	2	0	Bishop Auckland
Hartlepool Utd	1947-48	43	16	TR
Barnsley	1948-49	41	12	TR
West Bromwich Albion	1950-51	29	8	TR
Chester City	1951-52	23	6	TR
Hartlepool Utd	1952-55	106	24	TR

Interviewed April 2000

Fred Richardson was the type of player who would probably have made a fortune in today's game. He changed clubs on a number of occasions and passed up opportunities to play for Manchester United and Arsenal. In the days of the maximum wage there was less of an advantage for the big city clubs and not the same clamour to join the elite for a big pay day.

Having been spotted playing for Spennymoor Juniors, Fred was originally taken on by Newcastle United. Wor Jackie Milburn was amongst the luminaries at St. James' but Fred was not signed up and returned to play with Bishop Auckland. It was in the final of the FA Amateur Cup in 1946 where he got his big break. Bishops lost 2-3 to Barnet at Stamford Bridge but Fred was a star performer and was immediately snapped up by Chelsea. He was restricted to two League appearances with The Blues mainly because he was the understudy to the great Tommy Lawton. He would have loved to have stayed too. However, a few pints after a game were his downfall. He had been seen and reported to the Board who immediately stopped his wages. Fred was not amused and had a run-in with the Board, which resulted in his return north, much against the wishes of manager, Billy Birrell.

Hartlepool's Fred "The Tank" Richardson (centre) kills another goalkeeper in 1953

Hartlepool was the lucky recipient of the Richardson signature. He was a regular for just over a season and scored sixteen times for a struggling team. A number of clubs were keen to sign him, Arsenal amongst them. However, the sight of the Barnsley chairman arriving in a Rolls Royce to court him persuaded Fred that Oakwell was worth a try. Chilean international George Robledo had left Barnsley for Newcastle so £5,000 Fred was guaranteed a first team spot in a good Second Division team. He performed well at the higher level and was again targeted by First Division clubs. On this occasion, Fred was persuaded to move on to West Brom after being coveted by Sunderland. In a twist of fate, one of his first games was against The Rokermen at The Hawthorns. The Baggies won 3-0 with Fred scoring two and making the other.

He had been out injured for a while at West Brom after Arsenal's Leslie Compton jumped on his knee. Cortizone injections got him back on his feet. However, after one season in the top division he had a fall-out with manager Jack Smith. A player had shaken a bottle, which had fizzed up and spurted all over the manager. Fred found this particularly amusing. So much so that Smith never forgave him. He was soon on his way to Chester City where he played out a one year contract before moving back to Hartlepool and finishing his career playing for Fred Westgarth in the Third Division (North). During the close-seasons he would play cricket, which he continued well after his football days were over.

Fred's was a career that covered every League Division and included mixing it with some of the greatest names ever to grace the game. His League debut had been against Everton at Goodison Park. Colleagues had included Tommy Lawton at Chelsea and Danny Blanchflower and Tommy Taylor at Barnsley. He had played against Bobby Robson at Fulham and the player he admired most, John Charles at Leeds United. He had even got to know the soon-to-be cricket legend, Dickie Bird, a great Barnsley fan and had a young reporter regularly trying to cadge tickets from him - Michael Parkinson. His most treasured moments were the West Brom days in the First Division and he deeply regrets not making the dream move to Highbury when he had the chance. But his strong, bullish style served him well for ten League seasons.

Nowadays he resides in Coxhoe. He retired from the building trade some years ago and 'looked after' Thornley for a while after finishing with Hartlepool. Bowls is his game though the knees give him bother at times. As for football, he watches the TV and freely admits that after playing for £10 per week plus £2 win and £1 draw bonuses, he wishes he could have his time now to cash in on the extraordinary wealth of the modern game.

	Seasons	Apps	Goals	Source
Graham Richardson (G) Sedgefield, 20 March 1958 E U19				
Hartlepool Utd	1975-80	89	0	Darlington (Am)

Interviewed April 2000

Graham Richardson's ambition had always been to play in the Football League. Mission accomplished. In fact, mission accomplished eighty-nine times.

Born and bred in Sedgefield, he was originally on the ground staff at Darlington where he played a couple of friendlies as an amateur. He'd had trials for a number of clubs but had effectively to choose between Darlington and Middlesbrough. Choosing Darlington turned to his advantage when Billy Horner moved to Hartlepool and took Graham with him. He turned pro' at 17yrs and made his League debut in a 1-1 draw at Brentford in the 1975-76 season. It was a bruising encounter in which he was 'kicked all over' by opposing centre-forward Dave Simmons. Welcome to the Football League.

During the following five seasons he shared goalkeeping duties with, amongst others, Eddie Edgar, Barry Watling and John Hope. In his second term a knee ligament injury sustained against Whickham in the Wearside League, whilst playing for the reserves, was to cause him recurring problems that would restrict his appearances. However, he was on duty on that famous day in 1979 when United took on the might of First Division Leeds in the third

Graham Richardson turning out for Peterlee with a large moustache in 1988. (Photo: Hartlepool Mail)

FOOTBALL FOR ALL

5-a-side football
Indoor and outdoor leagues
Junior coaching
Advanced coaching
Soccer six tournaments
Ladies football

Outdoor pitches
Floodlit multi purpose areas
Training areas
280 seater grandstand and floodlit pitch
Changing Facilities

FOR INFORMATION AND BOOKINGS

SPENNYMOOR
LEISURE CENTRE
Tel:01388 815627

SHILDON SUNNYDALE
LEISURE CENTRE
Tel:01388 777340

NEWTON AYCLIFFE
LEISURE CENTRE
Tel:01325 300800

FERRYHILL
LEISURE CENTRE
Tel:01740 654123

Sedgefield BOROUGH LEISURE services

round of the FA Cup. Sixteen thousand fans crammed into the Victoria Ground, myself amongst them, to witness a gulf in class that was personified in Tony Curry's performance and the eventual 2-6 scoreline. This was Graham's personal highlight in his club career. However, it was not a great occasion for sportsmanship. It was a rough game and a '...war of words off the pitch'. Leeds weren't too pleased with the facilities.

Another personal highlight was representing his country. It is perhaps a little known fact that Graham played two games for the England under-19's team in the company of Glen Hoddle, Graham Rix, Alan Curbishley, Kevin Reeves, Tommy Langley and Aiden McCaffrey. Both matches were against Wales in a 'Little World Cup'. The first was a 1-0 victory and the second a 2-3 defeat at Maine road, Manchester that knocked England out of the competition. Is Graham Richardson the only player to represent England whilst on the Hartlepool books? We think he is.

Unfortunately, the 1980-81 season saw the premature end to his League career. A knee injury sustained at Crewe was treated less than sympathetically by the club. Billy Horner would not allow the trainer onto the pitch and Graham was forced to play with the injury in subsequent matches. He walked out at the end of the season, unwilling to put himself at further risk. He later made it up with Horner but the damage had been done. Subsequent seasons for Easington in the Wearside League and Peterlee and Spennymoor in the Northern represented his football finale.

The colleagues he admired most were Glen Hoddle from the England camp and Bob Newton at Hartlepool. He wasn't a great friend of Newton and felt he'd wasted his talent to a degree. Nevertheless, he was a good player. Opponents he admired were Luther Blisset and Ross Jenkins, the Watford duo and Robbie Jones, John Toshack and Alan Curtis of the emerging Swansea side. However, despite the memories, he doesn't miss the game at all. Since the age of twenty he'd played cricket for Hartlepool during the summer months and he still plays full seasons for them now batting in the middle order for the first or second eleven.

Work has been varied since he left the game. He had a Post Office at Seaham for six years and is now the area manager for a credit company. He still lives in Hartlepool and keeps in touch with the odd ex-colleague but is not nostalgic and has no regrets about his career. In fact he's enjoyed life since football and intends to continue doing just that.

	Seasons	Apps	Goals	Source
Joseph Roddom (WH)				
Spennymoor, 16 May 1924				
Chesterfield	1948	0	0	Blyth Spartans
Darlington	1950	6	0	TR

Joe Roddom didn't make his League debut until the ripe old age of twenty-six, an age at which many a career is long finished. He played six games at half-back in the Third Division (North) under the management of ex Crystal Palace goalkeeper, George Irwin following an initial spell at Second Division Chesterfield. They'd spotted him playing for Blyth Spartans in the North Eastern League, but the alliance yielded no senior appearances and Joe moved on to Feethams. His first appearance came in the second game of the season in front of a 14,000 crowd at Mansfield where The Quakers went down to a 1-2 defeat at the hands of the team who were to take the second promotion spot that season. His final League appearance was in the 1-6 drubbing at the hands of local rivals, Hartlepool in front of a 10,000 derby crowd on Good Friday, the home team being the happy beneficiaries of three penalty decisions. Joe had played his last game for Darlington.

R is for Referee

If you look in a dictionary or thesaurus and seek other words for a person performing a similar function to the 'man in the middle' you will come across terms like adjudicator or judge, arbitrator or mediator. These are people referred to for a decision in a dispute or a ruling against a set of laws. These are people of substance who command respect and help hold firm the consensual understanding of the need for structure and parameters in society. However, if you call such a person a referee and give him a whistle he becomes the most hated man on the planet for the ninety minutes that he plies his trade. You see, referees are not allowed to make mistakes. While goalkeepers blunder, strikers fluff, defenders step out at the wrong time and midfielders lose the plot, referees must remain infallible.

Such is the extent of peer pressure in the stands it can be difficult not to get caught up in the persecution of these brave but ultimately doomed men. Take the experience of Neil Midgely recalling in 1995 his First Division debut:

"My wife, who was in the stand, told me that at one stage the entire row in front of her stood up and gave me the v-sign. I asked her what she did and she said she didn't want them to know who she was so she stood up and joined in".....It's like Nazi Germany.

Mel Machin, the former Bournemouth manager seemed to be suggesting the final solution when he had two players sent of in 1995:

"If this had happened in a South American country, he'd have been shot at half time".

Now, it has to be said that some referees have not helped the cause. Take Paul Alcock's remarkable Michael Jackson moonwalk and comedy crumble to the turf after being wafted across the chest by Paulo Di Canio. Take Clive Thomas blowing the full-time whistle in a 'real' world cup match, Brazil v Sweden in 1978, as the ball is actually in mid-flight into the net. Goal disallowed. These were acts designed to bring derision and scorn upon the profession and support the notion in some quarters that referees are not, shall we say, in tune with the music of the modern game.

Certainly, Norman Whiteside was of that opinion:

"I never comment on referees and I'm not going to break the habit of a lifetime for that prat".

Mind you, there are moments that remind us that everyone is human. How can anyone fail to sympathise with referee Ian Borrett after his admission to Crystal Palace manager, Alan Smith in 1993:

"I'm having a crap match and nothing you can say will alter it".....Touche, Mr. Borrett.

The 'S' Team

	Seasons	Apps	Goals	Source
Arthur Sewell (IL) Cornforth, 15 July 1934 Bradford City (Am)	1954	1	0	Bishop Auckland

Like a number of Sedgefield's League performers, Arthur Sewell retained his amateur status whilst trying his hand with a professional club, in his case Bradford City. The 5' 9" inside-left was signed by manager Ivor Powell pre-season in June 1954, from Bishop Auckland of the Northern League. However, exactly one year later he was released, along with several other players, after playing only once in the Third Division (North). His debut and swansong came in the 1-1 draw at Valley Parade versus Chesterfield on the 13th November 1954.

	Seasons	Apps	Goals	Source
Barry Shaw (OL) Chilton, 31 October 1948 Darlington (Am)	1967	2	0	Crowboro Athletic

Interviewed February 2000

The anticipation of a career in football and the reality of it can often be very different. Many talented performers have reached the verge of the professional game only to find that circumstances conspire to push them in another direction.

Barry Shaw had been an outstanding junior at Aycliffe and Chilton appearing on one occasion as a 'wrong-un' for West Auckland in the Northern League. He caught the eye of Darlington Football Club and was persuaded to train there as a junior even playing a couple of reserve team games under the management of Jimmy Greenhalgh. However, Barry never displayed the burning ambition to become a professional and in fact turned down the opportunity for further trials at West Brom, Sheffield United and Blackpool instead preferring to complete his apprenticeship with the NCB. During this period he played for Crowboro Athletic, the Aycliffe factory side based at Chilton. However, Darlington kept tabs on him and in 1967 he was invited to train with the club again by the new manager, Ray Yeoman. He signed amateur forms and eventually made his League debut away at Newport County in the Fourth Division. The Northern Echo made much of his debut with a photo opportunity on the Friday before the game featuring Barry emerging black-faced from Metal Bridge drift mine ready to pull on his boots for The Quakers.

He played a further game at home to Rochdale but confesses that the whole episode was actually rather deflating. He didn't play particularly well in either match and along with two other amateurs, Kenny Felton and Chris Neal, felt unwelcome amongst the professional staff whose places they were competing for. Indeed one player used to attempt to bribe the amateurs to make him look good in training. It was a hard regime and a trying time which was ended when the management staff decided that with 23 professionals on the books they could not afford to have the amateurs taking first team shirts. Barry left to sign for Crook along with Chris Neal and his connection with League football was ended. He now lives in Kirk Merrington and follows the Boro for fun. Fun?

	Seasons	Apps	Goals	Source
Ronald Spence (WH)				
Spennymoor, 7 January 1927 Died 1996				
York City	1947-58	280	25	Rossington Colliery

Ron Spence remained in Yorkshire after leaving Spennymoor as a young man, his last team in the north east being Tudhoe Colliery. After signing for York City in March 1948 from Rossington Colliery, Bootham Crescent became his spiritual home for 27 years until 1975. His only break from the county capital was a three-year spell from the summer of 1960 when he spent three non-league seasons at Scarborough and Goole Town. In 1963 he returned to City as the club's part-time trainer, taking over the full-time role from Sid Storey in 1966.

York's Ron Spence looking like a no-nonsense half-back

As a player, Ron was regarded as one of one of York's most tireless servants and his twelve seasons of service earned him a richly deserved benefit match in 1955. As an attacking half-back, he had established himself as a first-team regular with his surging runs and indomitable spirit making him one of the club's most popular post-war players. The highpoint of his career was the 1955 FA Cup semi-final appearance against eventual winners Newcastle United. The team had rampaged through the competition beating Blackpool, Tottenham and Notts County as the season's giant killing act. At Hillsborough they almost did it again, drawing 1-1 with the star-studded Magpies in front of 65,000 fans. The dream was dashed in the Roker Park replay when they eventually surrendered 0-2 but City had captured the collective imagination of the nation with their cavalier attacking style. To date this remains the club's finest hour in the world's oldest competition.

A serious knee injury sustained against Barrow in March 1956 kept Ron out of the game for eighteen months and on his return in the 1957-58 season he had lost his edge. He appeared in the FA Cup games against Birmingham and Bolton but couldn't command a regular first team place. However, he stayed on for the promotion season of 1958-59 but his final League outing was in the 3-2 victory over Walsall in November 1958 and the subsequent move to non-league Scarborough was not unexpected.

On his return to Bootham in 1963 he began his career as a York City backroom boy that would see him as assistant trainer, physio' and youth team coach until he left football to join the licensed trade in 1975. After managing the Spitalbeck pub outside York, he took a pub in London but suffered a series of health problems that forced him to move back north. A stroke, a heart attack and a five-way heart by-pass operation preceded his death in Doncaster Infirmary in 1996. But he will always be remembered as one of the historic 1955 heroes in what was probably York City's most exciting team ever.

	Seasons	Apps	Goals	Source
Richard Steel (FB)				
Sedgefield, 13 March 1930				
Bristol City	1953-55	3	0	Ferryhill Athletic
York City	1956-57	3	0	TR

Richard 'Dickie' Steel was a highly rated amateur with Ferryhill Athletic before being spotted by Bristol City and taken to Ashton Gate by manager Pat Beasley in 1953. However, his first team opportunities were rare and although he was a member of the playing squad that won the Third

Division (South) Championship in 1955-56 he wasn't able to carve out a long-term career in Bristol.

Sam Bartram took him to York City in 1956 but again his first eleven chances were limited by a sitting member. George Howe had the left-back role almost permanently nailed down and Dickie was restricted to three appearances in the Third Division (North). His final League match was against Halifax at the Shay Ground in March 1958 in a 1-2 defeat. He was released from Bootham Crescent at the end of the season and continued a non-league career in the south-west with, amongst others, Merthyr Tydfil and Chippenham Town.

	Seasons	Apps	Goals	Source
Andrew Strong (LB)				
Trimdon, 17 September 1966				
Middlesbrough	1984	6	0	APP

Interviewed February 2000

The football record books show that Andrew Strong was born in Hartlepool, which indeed he was, in a hospital. In fact he is a Trimdon lad through and through. He was first taken on by Boro as a thirteen year-old and retained his association with the club for almost seven years as a schoolboy, apprentice and full-time professional.

The 'growing-up years' were spent in the company of Parkinson, Cooper, Currie, Pallister and Ripley amongst others. It was a talented reserve team that achieved a fair measure of success. However, he had to wait until April 1995 before making his full League debut in a 0-0 home fixture against Leeds United in the Second Division. This was the most exciting moment and the high point of a career at Ayresome Park that was unfortunately restricted to a further five games. Sheffield United, Man City, Wimbledon, Charlton and Carlisle followed but the arrival of Bruce Rioch, a strict disciplinarian, signalled the end for Andrew. Rioch came with a formidable reputation and a penchant for confrontation. The two did not hit

Andrew Strong (third up on the right) with several other reprobates in the all-conquering Sedgefield Comp' team of the late 70's. John Burton – the bloke at the back - watches over them.

it off. Andrew also recalls that fellow Trimdoner John Tinkler, also at Boro as a schoolboy, was never given a chance and spent most of his time doing menial tasks.

His next footballing assignment was altogether more glamorous as a Jamaican team took him for a couple of months in the sunshine. He was rewarded for his efforts with a free trip to the 1986 World Cup Finals in Mexico where he witnessed England's demise against Portugal. The 0-1 defeat included the sub-plots of Brian Robson dislocating a shoulder and Ray Wilkins being sent off for bouncing the ball at the referee. It was then back to wet and windy reality at Northern League Billingham Synthonia.

He had reason to believe his luck had changed in 1989 when a football agent took him and a number of other young pros to Belgium where he appeared for Roeseller Sporting Club based just outside Bruges. However, his two-year contract with the second division outfit turned sour when it emerged that the agent was cheating his charges of their wages. After losing several thousand pounds Andrew returned home half way through the contract. His professional career had effectively ended. It was a major disappointment but his lowest ebb came whilst at Boro when he suffered a freak injury in a reserve match played on a dodgy pitch, which had been covered with straw to protect it. Not all of the straw had been properly removed and when executing a sliding tackle one quill-like remnant of the pitch covering pierced his skin and lodged itself behind his knee. Over the coming weeks the deterioration of the muscles was a mystery until x-rays identified the culprit festering away in his leg. It was never really the same again.

He doesn't bother with the game now, especially since the shattering blow that fractured his shinbone in seven places in 1994; "...it snapped like a chicken bone". He keeps in touch with some of the old colleagues such as Tony McAndrew and John Tinkler but has never fancied coaching and professes to being a bad spectator. He's still living in Trimdon, working for Electrolux as we speak and happy to be found at The Royal in Trimdon Colliery for a recreational pint.

 **is for Shorts**

Ever since football was played in its league format, starting in 1888, the participants have always worn shorts. However, the humble short has been the focus of changing trends in kit design from that day to this. Indeed most football fans, shown a disembodied pair of legs clothed for action, would probably pick the era those legs were performing in simply by addressing the cut of the shorts.

Back in the late Victorian days of William MacGregor's fledgling Football League, the shorts worn by the founder members were more akin to the modern day peddle-pusher stretching from high on the waist-line to just above the knee; more of a cut-down trouser really. Team photographs from the era would often show the players posing as if for a Grattons catalogue shoot. Some would recline casually on the grass with one knee angled skyward, gazing wistfully into the middle distance whilst others would lean stylishly against a bench or wall with a hand poised on one hip or slipped into a pocket (yes, shorts with pockets). All, of course, had moustaches.

Even the pitch was different in those days. Up until 1902 the goalmouth consisted of two overlapping, six-yard semi-circles, one 'drawn' compass-style from each of the goal posts. From the air this looked like a giant backside. In 1901 the last Cup Final to be played with these pitch markings was won by Spurs, the only non-league team ever to win the trophy. The following year saw the field-of-play evolve to a style, which has remained almost unchanged to this day.

The next few years saw the shorts creeping further up the thigh and becoming baggier but it wasn't until the mid-twenties that they began to resemble the lighter, drawn-at-the-waist style that we imagine from the golden post-war era. At least they now looked asif they had been designed for their purpose. And when we got to the post-war period football shorts achieved levels of bagginess that could only have previously been dreamt of. This was the golden era for shorts.

As we entered the sixties the hemline rose rapidly and horrible substances like nylon started to make an appearance. Shirts also began to evolve into the tighter, round-necked version. With shorts now resting on the upper thigh rather than the knee there was now more leg on show than ever before. With the onset of the seventies shorts went from trim to skimpy, to obscene. Not only was there more leg on display but in some cases, particularly when the rolled waist band was deployed, the appearance was more of a bag of onions than a pair of football shorts. The 1980's were little better with Kevin Keegan continuing to be one of the biggest culprits.

It took the 90's to restore some order to the scene. The age of retro upon us, short design turned to the past for inspiration and baggy was back in. Thank God. However, since the seventies the addition of maker's marks and spooky patterns has given both shorts and shirts the added value of being a fashion item. The only problem is, there's only one way for shorts to go now, back up. Look out for more onion bags in about fifteen years time.

The 'T' Team

	Seasons	Apps	Goals	Source
John Tinkler (M)				
Trimdon, 24 August 1968				
Hartlepool Utd	1986-91	170	7	JNRS
Preston North End	1992	24	2	TR
Walsall (N/C)	1993	6	0	TR

Interviewed February 2000

Luck plays such a great part in the life of a professional footballer. Being in the right place at the right time can make a career. Getting a bad break can destroy it. And so it proved time and again for John Tinkler, another product of the Trimdon footballer factory of the mid-eighties who matured into an uncompromising midfielder who could also play football.

John Tinkler in 1988 ponders an alternative career if the football goes belly-up – modelling sunglasses. (Photo: Hartlepool Mail)

Things began brightly enough with a debut as sub' for Hartlepool at Cambridge as a seventeen-year-old junior followed by signing professional forms in 1987 and five seasons of regular first team football. There were numerous highlights such as the Quarter-Final of the Sherpa Van Trophy at Roker Park in early 1987 when 'Pools beat Sunderland, then Third Division leaders, 1-0. Then there was the second round League Cup tie at White Hart Lane in front of 19,000 fans when Spurs triumphed 5-0. A certain Paul Gascoigne scored four times with poor Steve Tupling given the unenviable task of man-marking him. Gazza was soon to leave for Lazio and the millionaires of Serie 'A'. Perhaps the proudest moments, however, were his short spell captaining the team and the promotion campaign of 1990/91 when 'Pools finished third behind Darlington and Stockport County. John's commemorative tankard is proof of the achievement. These were the days when Hartlepool trained where they could, the Power Station, Grayfields or The Mayfair Centre. Nowadays they have their fancy new academy and permanent training facilities at Peterlee.

However, after a spell in the Third Division with Hartlepool, John was transferred to Preston-North-End, also in that Division after falling out of favour with manager Alan Murray. It was in this later period at the Victoria Ground when his luck ran out and he was often in the wrong place at the wrong time. Take the famous Hardwick Hotel incident where John had been out for a Thursday night beer with a couple of the lads and spotted the club chairman, Gary Gibson who was there for similar purposes. John had only just arrived and was cold sober but he shouldn't have been there. Fearing Gibson had seen them, they high-tailed it out of town. Two weeks later, Alan Murray asked a seemingly innocent question about the movements of players in the week of the Hardwick visit. Assuming this was directed at him, John owned up to being out for a drink - 'a fair cop guv' - and Murray gleefully accepted the confession, fined him and banned him from the club for a week. In fact, Gibson hadn't seen them at all and Murray was non-the-wiser until John piped up. The wrong place at the wrong time.

Previously, John's good form for Hartlepool had caught the collective eye of Dundee in the Scottish Premiership. John Brown made a [technically illegal] approach to John by telephone stating that he was about to offer £80,000 for him, was he interested? Was he ever? Three weeks later, manager Bob Moncur notified him that there had been a £70,000 bid from Dundee and he would be informing the board but advising them to turn it down at that price. A week later, John broke his ankle in a night match at Halifax at a time when Everton and Crystal Palace were also showing interest. Wrong place at the wrong time.

Then of course, there was the match video that was sent to all top division clubs as a shop window for the 'Pool players. John picked up an injury before the game and was replaced by Don Hutchison who was subsequently signed by the Anfield boss, Kenny Dalglish. Hutchison, a man in the right place at the right time. As a side issue, this was a deal borne of the legendary negotiation at which chairman Gibson had been determined to hold out for a £5,000 signing on fee and a £300 per week wage deal for the player. When he arrived at Anfield he was faced with an intransigent club unwilling to deviate from their once and only offer of £500 per week and a £25,000 signing on fee. Gibson 'gave in' and the deal was done.

John's spell at Preston ended when he was frozen out by the new manager, John Beck of long-ball fame and forced to train with the youth team. After one year of a two-year contract he was released and took up the offer of a trial period at Walsall in the Third Division (this was the first year of the Premiership). It was a calculated gamble aimed at staying in League football but it was at the expense of an excellent offer from non-league Gateshead. Keith Nobbs, a former team-mate at Hartlepool became the beneficiary of that contract and when things didn't work out at Fellows Park John found himself on the road to Gateshead Stadium on a contract inferior to the one he had initially been offered.

So, after seven seasons and 200 League games John Tinkler turned to the non-league scene at Bishop Auckland, Fleetwood, Spennymoor, Prudhoe, Durham, Blyth and Morpeth. It's been a career of many ups, downs and what-ifs with perhaps the biggest regret being that he missed out on playing in the Scottish Premier League. However, he got to play against the great Gazza and was proud to name Rob McKinnon and Don Hutchison amongst his colleagues, the two best players he turned out with.

Still dwelling in Trimdon, he's now to be found working as a repair technician for Samsung at Wynyard as well as pulling on the pads and wielding the willow in spectacular fashion on the local cricket scene.

	Seasons	Apps	Goals	Source
Mark Tinkler (M)				
Byers Green, 24 October 1974	E Sch/E yth			
Leeds United	1992-1996	25	0	YT
York City	1996-1999	90	8	TR
Southend United	1999-2000	56	1	TR
Hartlepool United	2000-	28	3	TR

Mark Tinkler was an outstanding schoolboy footballer who captained England Schools to victory in the UEFA under-18 championship and also played in the junior team that included Ben Roberts, Rob Bowman and Adam Reed, all of whom would become professionals. He also attended the Manchester United regional school of excellence. However, it was Leeds United that finally pinned him down and he also captained the United team that lifted the FA Youth Cup, a precursor to making his first team debut aged eighteen. A promising start to his career in The Premiership was cut short by a broken leg suffered in a reserve match against Manchester United in 1983. Out for five months and rather apprehensive about the injury on his return, things were never quite the same at Elland Road after that.

The arrival of George Graham to take over from Howard Wilkinson in 1996 spelled the end for Mark who didn't figure in the new manager's plans. He wanted first team football and was granted a transfer, £85,000 to York City in March 1997. He spent two and a half seasons as a Bootham Crescent regular in the Second Division under manager Allan Little, then followed his boss to Southend United for £40,000 when Little moved to Roots Hall in the Third Division. However, Mark fell from the financial tightrope that small clubs are often forced to walk. Southend had to reduce their wage bill and a free transfer to Hartlepool was the outcome. A tremendous season for both Mark and the team followed, spoilt only by the agony of losing out on promotion in the end-of-season play-offs.

Mark Tinkler has just remembered that he's forgotten to take his vest off

For a man who's tasted life in The Premiership, returning to the glamour of the top flight remains the burning ambition. He's disappointed at the way things turned out at Leeds and George Graham is hardly his favourite person. But Mark Tinkler remains hopeful that at twenty-eight, there's still time.

	Seasons	Apps	Goals	Source
Michael Trotter (D/M)				
Trimdon, 27 October 1969				
Middlesbrough	1987	0	0	YTS
Doncaster Rovers	1988	3	0	L
Darlington	1990-91	29	2	TR
Leicester City	1991-92	3	0	TR
Chesterfield	1993	15	1	TR

Interviewed April 2000

Another Trimdon boy who made it to the pro' ranks, Michael Trotter was a youth team regular with Pallister, Mowbray and Ripley amongst others. Brian Little and Eddie Gray were coaching the youths in the promotion days of Rioch and Todd and under the cloud of liquidation with Middlesbrough chairman, Charles Amer. Those were the days when the players had to go to the Town Hall to pick up their pay. Michael particularly remembers when the gates were eventually closed on the club and the players dashed around to salvage as much training kit as possible before the padlock snapped shut.

He signed pro' forms in 1988 after a good run in the Youth Cup and subsequently appeared regularly for the reserves. However, it was difficult to break into the first team with Pallister, Mowbray and Kernaghan ahead of him in the pecking order. It was during this period that he embarked on a one-month loan period at Fourth Division Doncaster Rovers under the great Dave Mackay. A 1-0 home victory against Burnley in 1988 was Michael's League debut. He played a further two matches before returning to Boro' and the reserve team. However, he'd enjoyed his brief taste of first team football. Mackay was 'a good bloke' and Jackie Ashurst and Gerry Daly were a great influence on the field of play.

In 1990 Colin Todd, who had replaced the sacked Rioch, offered him a new two-year contract. However, Brian Little, with whom he had always stayed in touch, had moved on to Darlington and offered Michael the chance to join him and play first team football. He joined a winning team that went on to achieve promotion to the Third Division in May 1991 and he became the proud recipient of a championship winners' medal. It was a great atmosphere at the club with a blend of youth and experience. Andy Toman, Mick Tait and Frank Gray were amongst the happy crew. Tait was the hardest bloke he ever saw. Most importantly though, Michael was enjoying his football where he played mainly in midfield. Owen Willoughby who had taken him to Boro' initially, described him as 'a cultured player who could strike the ball beautifully'. Perhaps this was his best position really.

Brian Little was soon poached by Leicester City and bound for bigger things. He had a good rapport with Michael and took him to Filbert Street with Jimmy Willis. He had started the season at Feethams keeping Gary Gill out of the team but now found himself at a club heading for the Second Division play-off final, which they lost 0-1. The following season, his first full term at Leicester, saw the club reach the final yet again only to go down 3-4 to a Swindon team with Hoddle and Hazzard. On both occasions he was in the squad at Wembley but didn't get on to the pitch. He had two and a half years at the club making three League appearances but was never quite at the front of the queue for a centre-back position although ironically he played midfield for the reserves.

Two short loan periods preceded an end-of-season free transfer to Chesterfield under John Duncan. He signed a one-year deal and scored on his debut. Unfortunately a stand-up row with the manager over an on-the-pitch incident cost him dearly. Duncan took exception and that was his Chesterfield career up the spout. To add insult to injury, Duncan denied him a promised free transfer in the close season. This made it difficult for Michael to make an immediate move and he spent the next few weeks playing trial matches at Hereford, Hartlepool and Colchester. The Hartlepool experience was particularly unlucky since John MacPhail would have signed him had he not had his financial wings clipped as he attempted to strengthen the squad.

Still living in Leicester, Michael decided to try the foreign agents. In September 1994 he was whisked off to Hong Kong where he had three months with Frankwell Holdings in a league not unlike The Conference. It was a terrific experience, including a trip to China but he decided it wasn't the right long-term move for him and his wife so he returned home in November. Back on the trial circuit, he played a game for Walsall against Halifax. The hope was that Chris Nicholl would take him to the Bescot Stadium but while that door closed another opened in the shape of an offer to sign for John Bird at Conference side, Halifax. He signed and stayed for two and a half years and thoroughly enjoyed his time at The Shay where he was part of the Halifax revival. However, after Bird was sacked, he clashed over tactics with new manager, John Carroll and left the club. So, in 1996 he was looking for work again. On this occasion it was VS Rugby in the Beezer Homes League who came in for him. However, there were eventually problems with paying players' wages and although Michael was on a part-time contract he was glad he had taken up a position with The Royal Mail before leaving Halifax.

He continued with VS Rugby after taking employment as Football in the Community Officer at Leicester City but eventually had to give up playing as it began to clash with his work for the FA. By the end of 1999 he was finding it difficult to juggle football, work and personal life so made the decision to return to The Royal Mail as a postman and quit playing. Things have settled down now and he still keeps fit enough to make him think about getting back into the game, perhaps in a coaching capacity.

It would be easy for Michael to look back on his career and bemoan some bad luck and missed opportunities. However, he regrets nothing. It was a shame things didn't work out at Middlesbrough after such a long association but he had some good times and played with great colleagues such as Bernie Slaven and Gary Pallister. He had the immense thrill of winning a championship medal at Darlington and playing against the Manchester United starlets, Beckham, Scholes et al scoring two goals in a reserve match against them at Old Trafford. All things considered, he'd do it all again.

is for Talent

Talent is that most elusive of qualities. That great German utility man of letters Johann Wolfgang von Goethe observed that 'talent develops in quiet places, character in the full current of human life'. Even where it exists, it is often locked away, hidden, disguised by diffidence, shrouded by shyness or sometimes, simply unrecognised. Professional footballers have talent. Professional sportsmen and women of any persuasion have talent. Opera singers, dentists, artists and hairdressers all have talent. The trick is to spot that talent then draw it out, nurture it and set it free. For some there is no mystery. George Best had talent, everyone knew it, he knew it. But even George had to work hard to make sure that other components such as fitness, hunger and commitment were added to the core ingredient to create a recipe that tasted as good as any before or since. Talent isn't always enough.

On the football field talent is usually the word used to describe the more flamboyant skills that grace the game. Think of the slick trickery of Rodney Marsh or the hypnotic wizardry of Stanley Matthews. Think of the dead ball magic of David Beckham, the mystical French feet of David Ginola or the unfathomable sorcery of Gazza. These are the people who come most readily to mind as being gifted with footballing talent. However, if we take the dictionary definition of talent as 'a special aptitude or gift', then it becomes possible to recognise special aptitudes in most players. Bobby Moore, for instance, could not be described as having the power of Bobby Charlton or the unerring eye for goal of Jimmy Greaves but he could read a game, time a tackle, confound an attack better than any player that ever kicked a ball. That is talent. Then there are players like Alex Ferguson who clearly had a certain level of ability to play Scottish League football but who found that his real aptitude is in managing others, discovering talent in quiet places and developing it in the full current of human, or at least footballing life.

Then, of course, there is Billy Ashcroft, a Wrexham and Middlesbrough defender and centre forward with an afro haircut that would not have disgraced The Jackson Five. He could score a header from the eighteen-yard line with what amounted to a cushion on his head. Now that's talent. And what about Bernie Slaven, an Irish international with a Scottish accent who will forever be remembered for showing his arse in Binns window. Now ask yourself if you would be remembered throughout the country if you performed such an act. Now that's talent.

In fact, it seems to me that you can just about describe anything as a talent if you have enough imagination and it is possible to persuade people that you have talent even when you haven't. Just say it with confidence. Come to think of it, that's a talent in itself. Just ponder on the words of Winthrop Mackworth Praed who had a talent for humerous verse:

Of science and logic he chatters
As fine and as fast as he can;
Though I am no judge of such matters,
I'm sure he's a talented man.

U is for Ubiquitous

The 'U' Team

There is no League player from the Sedgefield area whose name begins with U. However, there was the Irish goalkeeper who played for Swindon, Portsmouth and Southend who went by the name of Norman Uprichard. I'm sure there's a joke there somewhere.

Seemingly omnipresent.

They're everywhere those ubiquitous types. You just can't avoid them wherever you turn. Take Juliet Morris for instance. There was a time when she was on every other television programme transmitted across these sceptered isles. And what of Carol Vorderman? She's gone one better and actually is on every programme on the goggle box. These are truly ubiquitous beings capable of being in several places at one time. Or perhaps human cloning techniques have advanced further than we have been led to believe and we are in fact witnessing a real life, real time experiment with a TV presenter who is actually a multiple. Next time you see her on TV look out for a man in a white coat in the background taking notes on a clipboard.

Football is full of these ubiquities. Take Alan Ball - as Portsmouth fans have said on more than one occasion - a great, great player but a manager who has moved from job to job over the years despite an unwavering ability to deliver failure. His ubiquity has faded of late but there was a time when he was everywhere, squeaking into the camera about the latest crisis he was embroiled in.

Mark Lawrenson is the latest of the media pundits to have taken over the world. To make matters worse he's also a favourite subject of impressionist, Alistair McGowen. So if we are not being offered the wise words of the original and genuine article, we're being treated to a version of it, which in some ways is more realistic than the real thing.

The big problem with Lawrenson is that he is yet another ex-Liverpool player expected to be objective when it comes to discussing The Premiership. Think about it - Lawrenson, Hansen, Barnes and Venison on TV. Then on the radio there's Steve McMahon, Jan Molby, Jim Beglin and David Fairclough - oh and of course, Lawrenson. Ubiquitous Liverpool.

Then there's that bloke I sat next to at the match the other week. He gets louder and louder as the game progresses and as he sips whisky from a badly concealed hip flask. The language deteriorates into the industrial variety and the abuse of his team develops to the point of being irrational, even slightly psychotic. He goes completely bananas when the manager substitutes the one player who seems to be making an impression on the opposition. He's on his feet berating the bench and inventing new and exciting ways to verbally abuse his fellow man when the six blokes in front turn round as one and wearily state what is obvious to all but our resident nutcase. "He's injured." The ubiquitous basket case is the reason I would never buy a season ticket. Can you imagine sitting next to that for a whole season?

Finally, there is the ubiquitous club mascot. Usually this is a 'fan' dressed in an animal suit and a club kit with an inane name like Cyril the Swan. He will lap the pitch waving to the stands and shaking hands with frightened school children in the front row. It's just too much.

The 'V' Team

	Seasons	Apps	Goals	Source
John (Jack) Vitty (FB)				
Chilton, 19 January 1923				
Charlton Athletic	1946	2	0	Boldon Villa
Brighton & H.A.	1949-51	47	1	TR
Workington	1952-56	196	3	TR

Interviewed March 2000

During 1948 the three Vitty brothers found themselves in the unusual, and up to that time, unique situation of being on the books of the same club at the same time. Jim was a pro' but never made a League appearance, Ron went on to make a handful of appearances for Hartlepool and Jack carved out a nine-season career as a solid and dependable fullback. All three had their opportunities reduced by the war, which effectively delayed their professional playing days.

They were all on the books at First Division Charlton Athletic under manager, Jimmy Seed who spent twenty-two years in charge at The Valley from 1935 onwards. The forties were the most successful years in the club's history with top-flight football and consecutive Cup Finals in 1946 and 1947 so the brothers had joined a high-flying outfit. Such was the quality at the club that Jack was only able to force his way into the first team on two League occasions. His debut was in a 1-5 defeat at the hands of Derby County at The Baseball Ground and his second game, a 2-2 draw at Villa Park brought him up against the legendary, Tommy Lawton. He played a lot of reserve team football but also suffered an injury that restricted his chances and regular fullbacks Jackie Shreeve and Frank Lock proved difficult to dislodge. Mind you, reserve games in those days could be spectacular affairs. Jack recalls performing in front of 67,000 fans in a reserve encounter with Arsenal.

Jack Vitty (left) looks on in disbelief as the referee shakes hands with The League's smallest captain
(Photo: Ivor Nicholas)

He spent three years with Charlton up to 1949 on wages of £8 per week in winter and £5 in the summer but had played football during the war representing The Royal Marines against The Army and playing for the Combined Services. They played in exotic places such as India and Ceylon and Jack admits that he saw little action because of his football activity. His good fortune in that department held for D-Day as brother Jim was active in the landings while Jack was on leave.

Following the Charlton days, ex-Valley player Don Welsh took the manager's job at The Goldstone Ground, Brighton and paid Charlton £3,000 to take Jack with him. He spent two seasons at the Third Division (South) club but fell out of favour with new manager, Billy Lane in 1951. Jack regarded him as a 'nasty piece of work' who clearly wanted him out. It was a shame since he had made good friends amongst the players and would have liked to have stayed. However, it wasn't to be and he was eventually sold for £750 to Workington Town where he soon developed a great rapport with the local fans. It was here that he encountered the best manager he ever came across, the great Bill Shankly, who made Jack team captain. He was a master tactician, an inspirational motivator, a man of great depth of feeling and someone who could 'make you feel six feet tall'. And unusually for a manager, he never swore. He was simply the very best.

The Vitty family was made to feel at home by the townsfolk and threw themselves whole-heartedly into the life of the community even becoming members of the local Amateur Operatic Society. On the field, Jack helped the club climb gradually from second bottom of The League in 1952-53 to fourth position in 1956-57 whilst becoming the first 'Reds' player to make 100 first class appearances. As a natural leader, he was noted for his manner with young players and performed many extra-curricular duties in the town as a representative of the club including coaching local school children.

After a distinguished career with Workington, Jack left the club at the age of thirty-five having picked up an achilles injury against Rotherham from which he never really recovered. New manager, Norman Low released him and he returned to South Shields where he had grown up and been a school friend of the great Stan Mortenson. He played for Shields and finally for the club where it had all started, Boldon Villa. He subsequently became a chemical plant engineer doing a stint in Saudi Arabia before returning to Eaglescliffe where he lived until retirement and a third return to South Shields. He still watches football and is a keen Sunderland fan particularly of the partnership between Phillips and Quinn. However, he is worried about the impact of money on today's game and the effect it will have on smaller clubs. He missed playing when he finished and although he did some scouting for Joe Harvey he didn't really fancy management. So he allowed himself to leave the game behind in order to forge an alternative career and is now able to look back with satisfaction - "it's a great game and I was pleased to have been in it. It was a good job."

	Seasons	Apps	Goals	Source
Ronald Vitty				
Chilton, 18 April 1927				
Charlton Athletic	1947	0	0	Boldon Villa
Hartlepool Utd	1949	6	0	TR
Bradford City	1950	0	0	TR

Interviewed March 2000

Ron was the third of the Vitty brothers to be captured by Charlton Athletic boss, Jimmy Seed. He was signed 'unseen' by the manager after Jim and Jack had convinced Seed that there was another brother on the conveyor belt. He recalls arriving at 11.00pm and sleeping the night on the trainer's bench in a blacked out Valley. He was rewarded for his endeavours with a £7 per week contract and stayed two and a half years before moving on to Hartlepool.

He was a full-time pro' but didn't quite make The League eleven for the 'Addicks', spending most of his time in the reserves. In fact, his first match at Charlton was for the reserves at Fratton Park, Portsmouth with brother, Jack at right-back and Ron at left-back.

His signing as a pro' followed a promising period as a junior at Marsden, a welding apprenticeship in the Jarrow steelworks and service for his country in the war. He had been in the Royal Navy and saw action in the Far East with deep-sea minesweepers. However, he didn't really like London and when the opportunity arose for a free transfer, a move to Hartlepool at last gave him the chance of League football. Fred Westgarth took him to the Victoria Ground where he played six times in the Third Division (North). The last of those matches was against New Brighton at the Tower Grounds the year before they failed to gain re-election to The League and began a sad decline into oblivion, which ended in their eventual extinction in 1983. As for Ron, he was transferred to Bradford City in 1950 but never made a League appearance after breaking a leg in the close season. He had been out on a run, had slipped and fallen on a level crossing in Boldon and as he lay on the ground the crossing gates closed preventing a bus from doing more serious damage to him. A policeman carried him from the tracks and ferried red-faced Ron to hospital.

A three-month trial with York was an attempt to revive the career but he eventually threw in the towel and signed for North Shields to continue his football in a non-league setting. Work with the Triplex Safety Glass people took him to Birmingham where he settled down, had a son and daughter and retired in 1990 aged sixty-three.

His best football memories were his appearance at Highbury and winning the 'All Good Causes' Cup for Charlton Athletic versus Slough. However, he believes he could, perhaps should have made more of his talent. In his own words, " I was a bit of a silly lad and didn't take it seriously. But I did enjoy the game."

V is for Vision

Vision in a footballer is a gift to be treasured. The ability to see a pass, to predict the run of a team-mate, to see the keeper off his line or to split a defence. Vision is the secret ingredient, the unwritten family formula, the exotic mix of spices that, added to the football recipe, turns a satisfying meal into a mouth-watering feast.

Kevin Keegan once said of David Ginola, "He has pace, trickery and vision. You're not supposed to have all three." That's what made Ginola a mouth-watering feast and one of the players who will be talked about for years after he has finished with the game.

Players with true vision on the field of play are long remembered by the fans and can also make colleagues better players than they would otherwise have been. Peter Beardsley is the classic example of a man whose footballing wit and vision was such a huge influence on Gary Lineker and Andy Cole amongst others. There are also those whose on-field vision leads them to do the most extraordinary things. Take the David Beckham goal from inside his own half that so stunned the Wimbledon crowd and propelled him to superstardom. The question there is not 'how many players would have attempted that shot?' No, the question is 'how many players would have even seen it as an option?'

But it's not just on the field of play that football produces men of vision, of imagination and foresight. Many a manager, chairman, player or commentator has taken it upon himself to wax lyrical on the beloved game producing pearls of wisdom that, if strung together, would grace the neck of any female football presenter - even Gabby Logan.

The Chairman: Peter Hill-Wood saw the future in 1982 when he claimed with confidence, "We will never again in this country see a club pay £1 million for a player."

The Retired Pro': In 1989 Alan Ball speaking on his future career was rather optimistic with his ambitions. "I always wanted to be the greatest player and got somewhere near to that. Now I want to be the greatest coach and manager in the country."

The Manager: Graham Taylor played Mystic Meg in 1989 when he accurately predicted, "Arsenal will either win or lose the championship this year."

The Coach: Fransisco Maturana, coach of the 1994 Columbian national side spoke with passion and vision about the role of football in his troubled country on the eve of the World Cup finals. " Through football we're trying to show that Columbia is about more than cocaine, violence, terrorism and death." His captain, Andres Escobar was later shot dead after making a mistake in a World Cup match.

The Player: In 1995 Gary Lineker was happy to quote his former manager Gordon Milne who had the vision to see that the modern footballer must adopt a moral stance in the face of all manner of abuses from the public. "If someone in the crowd spits at you, you've just got to swallow it."

The 'W' Team

	Seasons	Apps	Goals	Source
Dennis Walker (F)				
Spennymoor, 5 July 1948				
West Ham Utd	1966	0	0	APP
Luton Town	1967	1	0	TR

Dennis Walker's first opportunity to 'make it' with a top club came with Ron Greenwood at West Ham in the heady days of Upton Park when Moore, Peters and Hurst formed the backbone of the England world Cup winning side. Not surprising then that it was difficult to make a mark. He was released after one season as an apprentice and picked up on a two-month trial by Luton Town. The team from Kenilworth Road, managed by Allan Brown, would go on to win the Fourth Division Championship that year. However, Dennis's brush with the big time lasted only twelve minutes when he came on as a late substitute in a 2-0 victory over Barnsley in 1967. Obviously, he didn't do enough for Brown and he was released. None of our Sedgefield District footballers had a shorter League career but at least Dennis Walker got to drink from the same tea trolley as some of England's World Cup legends.

	Seasons	Apps	Goals	Source
Paul Ward (M)				
Fishburn, 15 September 1963				
Chelsea	1981	0	0	APP
Middlesbrough	1982-85	76	1	TR
Darlington	1985-87	124	9	TR
Leyton Orient	1988-89	31	1	TR
Scunthorpe Utd	1989-90	55	6	TR
Lincoln City	1990-92	39	0	TR

Interviewed March 2000

After a long and much-travelled playing career it is perhaps ironic that Paul Ward's claim to fame is as a manager. He was and still is the youngest ever League manager, taking over for three months at Darlington from the sacked Cyril Knowles. He was only twenty-three and had the additional burden of holding down a regular first team position. However, when the job was advertised on a permanent basis, Dave Booth was appointed ahead of him but the experience sowed the seeds of desire to become a manager later in his career.

It all began for Paul when Geoff Hurst, the nice cop to Boby Gould's bad cop, took him on as an apprentice with

Paul Ward (centre), and his Orient colleagues celebrate promotion in 1989 by offering their rendition of YMCA

Chelsea before spending a year as a full-time pro' under new manager, John Neal. Playing up front in those days, he was packed off to New Zealand for six months of first team experience with Columbus Waterside where John Fashanu was undergoing a similar blooding. However, when he returned John Neal had signed a couple of more experienced forwards and Paul's chances were always likely to be limited. Nevertheless, it was a tremendous learning period for the young Fishburn lad. Pro's such as Gary Stanley, Ian Britton, Clive Walker and Peter Rhodes-Brown were all admirable examples to the fresh apprentices but it was club captain, Micky Droy and Ray Wilkins who were 'Kings of The Bridge'. They had total respect from players and managers alike being addressed as 'Mister' by those outside the first-team squad and often acting as intermediaries in contract negotiations for the youngsters. Paul was in fact Micky Droy's boot boy; a job that had to be done just so or coach, Bobby Gould would fine the culprits anything up to a week's wages. In those days senior pro was a highly respected position and it was a major achievement to break into the first-team dressing room. You had to establish yourself in the reserves before having the temerity to challenge for the elite squad so gaining his first ever squad number '40' was a proud moment for Paul.

Unfortunately, although he appeared in first-team friendlies, he never made the first League eleven at Stamford Bridge. However, salvation came when scout Owen Willoughby, who had kept tabs on his progress since a boy, inquired about the possibility of taking Paul to Middlesbrough. He scored in a two-nil trial match victory at Blyth Spartans and was duly signed by The Boro. His League debut came in a 1-1 draw at St. James' Park in front of around 30,000 fans with Kevin Keegan and the on-loan Mick Channon on the opposing side. It was a memorable occasion.

These were the days of Pallister, Darren Wood, Heine Otto and Irving Nattrass all of whom he admired greatly. However, perhaps the best of them all was Stephen Bell, the prodigious talent that was never quite fulfilled. Paul believes that he probably had too much too soon and went of the rails somewhat. The England Youth international winger could have been one of the greats. One of the great characters of the team and a quality player, was Archie Stephens who was introduced to the club as 'Big Archie'. Not surprisingly everyone was expecting a giant, which he wasn't. But when the cry came from Maddren on the touchline, "bang it up for Archie", he could rise to head the ball against the best of them.

Paul played under Bobby Murdoch, Malcolm Alison, " a great man manager" and Willie Maddren at Ayrsome Park and it was Maddren who eventually decided that he should leave when Mitch Cook became available from Darlington. The Boro boss swapped Cook for Paul Ward and Alan Roberts and a new phase of his career began at Feethams. In his own words he "...loved my time at Darlington." Unfortunately, one of the lowest points of his career occurred at Darlington when a promised move to his boyhood idols, Sunderland fell through. Dennis Smith had agreed the deal, including personal terms but inexplicably changed his mind at the last minute leaving Paul to read the devastating news on the back page of the Northern Echo.

It was during the 1987 close season whilst attending a sportsman's dinner with Jeff Clarke and John Brownlie, that journalist, John Fotheringham of the Weekly News let it be known to Frank Clarke, then managing Orient, that Paul Ward was the man he needed at Brisbane Road. When Paul arrived back from his summer holidays there was indeed an offer from Clarke to Darlington boss, Dave Booth and the player was soon on the move again with a £15,000 fee written into the contract. His one season in the capital ended in promotion to the Third Division via the play-offs but he was soon on his way again with a move north to Scunthorpe under manager, Mick Buxton. A season and a half at The Old Showground was followed by a move to his final League club, Lincoln City in 1990. However, this was to end in the agony of a cruciate ligament injury sustained during a Coca Cola Cup tie against Doncaster Rovers in 1992. He had been playing on the left wing that night as opposed to his normal midfield anchor role. The move had disastrous consequences and Paul officially left the club in 1994 after a series of failed attempts to regain fitness.

A couple of enquiries from Burnley and Grimsby came in the later stages at Lincoln but his League days were over. Employment as youth team coach at Doncaster followed as did spells at a number of non-league clubs eventually culminating in his acceptance of the manager's job with Harrogate Town in the Unibond League Division One. However, despite a certain amount of success in his seven months, he was sacked by the chairman after a difference of opinion. He took the club to an industrial tribunal ...and won. It was a sobering experience but it hasn't put him off management. But for now he's earning a living from the two private members' gyms run by he and his wife. They've been established now for three years and business is fine, thanks. But football is still the first love and he'd like to get back into management. After all, it would be a shame if the League's youngest ever manager didn't add to his historic three month spell back in 1987.

	Seasons	Apps	Goals	Source
Geoffrey Wardle (WH)				
Trimdon, 7 January 1940				
Sunderland	1958	0	0	Houghton Jnrs
Lincoln City	1961	1	0	TR

Geoffrey Wardle was a professional Rokerman for three years under manager Alan Brown in the Second Division. However, he failed to make the necessary impact to break into the first team and eventually signed for Lincoln City manager Bill Anderson in 1961. His one and only appearance for 'The Red Imps' came at Sinal Bank on 14th October 1961 when he deputised for the ex-Middlesbrough full-back Ray Barnard. Thereafter, he left League football and remained in the area forging a non-league career with Kings Lynn, Matlock and Spalding.

	Seasons	Apps	Goals	Source
Charles Wayman (CF)				
Chilton, 16 May 1922				
Newcastle United	1946-47	47	32	Spennymoor Utd
Southampton	1947-49	100	73	TR
Preston North End	1950-54	157	104	TR
Middlesbrough	1954-55	55	31	TR
Darlington	1956-57	23	14	TR

Charlie Wayman was one of *the* great goalscorers. He notched an astonishing 254 successes in 382 League appearances, a 66% strike-rate which most international forwards would kill for. Like many of his generation, however, he missed out on even more appearances and goals because of the suspension of The League during the war years. Signed by Newcastle in 1941, he had to wait five seasons before making his League debut.

But it was during his south coast days at Southampton that he made a major impact on the footballing public. He was the Darling of The Dell following his five goals for The Saints against Leicester City in 1948 which had commentators calling for him to be capped by England. Unfortunately, the international call never came but the call from Deepdale did. Will Scott, the Preston-North-End manager secured his services to play along side the great Tom Finney.

Up to this point in his career, Charlie had played all of his football in the upper reaches of the Second Division. However, Preston was a major force at the time pressing to get back into the top division. In 1950-51 that ambition was realised when North End swept into Division One as Champions. The next three seasons would be the pinnacle of Charlie's career as he rubbed shoulders with England's finest and on two occasions topped the Division One scoring charts. He was one of the very best. Preston narrowly lost out to Arsenal in 1952-53 when The Gunners beat them to The Championship on goal average and suffered again in the Cup Final of 1953-54. On that occasion West Brom triumphed 3-2 but Charlie does have the memory of scoring a Wembley goal and shaking the hand of the Queen Mum before collecting his loser's medal.

The elder Wayman brother finished his football back in his native North-East with three seasons at Ayresome Park and Feethams before calling it a day at the age of thirty-five. He's a modest man who prefers not to talk about his achievements; they're quite capable of speaking for themselves. Now, sadly afflicted by long-term illness, he lives in Coundon secure in the knowledge that he made an indelible mark on the English Football League.

	Seasons	Apps	Goals	Source
Franklyn Wayman (OR)				
Chilton, 30 December 1931				
Preston North End	1953	0	0	
Chester City	1955	30	2	TR
Darlington	1957	1	0	Easington Colliery

Interviewed March 1995

Frank Wayman is the younger brother of Charlie and as happy to talk at length as his brother is to keep his counsel. If he didn't represent his country on the field of play, he could surely talk for England.

He followed his more illustrious sibling into the cutthroat world of League football at Preston North End in 1953-54 when Charlie was at the height of his powers. Frank was balancing a potential football career with life in the RAF based at Chester but he never quite made the Preston first

Frank and Charlie Wayman take a bath in their Preston days – the rest of the team are in there looking for the soap. (Photo: Provincial Press Agency)

team. Instead, he had to content himself with training in the company of those legendary Toms, Finney and Docherty. He summed them up thus; one was a 'gentleman' and the other a 'shit-house'. Go on then, which was which?

The move to Chester City in 1955 suited his personal and domestic circumstances whilst also giving him the taste of first team action in the Third Division (North). He was no mean performer though perhaps lacking the commitment of his older brother and it has to be said, he bore a striking resemblance to Jimmy Greaves. Though at five feet three and a half inches, he was a tad shorter. One newspaper report told of how Frank 'dumbfounded the home side's 'keeper' with a lob calmly placed over the Darlington goalie, Dunn. Perhaps there was a hint of Greavesie in front of goal as well as in front of the camera.

The RAF kept him in Chester before he finally finished his League career at Darlington, also with Charlie, after a brief spell at Easington. Frank was not enamoured by The Quakers whom he described as being so tight they wouldn't even pay your bus-fare. Nevertheless, he continued playing on the non-league scene with some distinction, content that he had graced the League stage, albeit briefly. As he sits at home in Chilton, he can perhaps recall with some satisfaction the programme notes from Rhyl v Chester City in the fifth round of the Welsh Cup in January 1956 which described him as 'the complete winger'. Praise indeed.

	Seasons	Apps	Goals	Source
Kenneth Whitfield (CH)				
Spennymoor, 24 March 1930 Died 1995				
Wolverhampton Wanderers	1951-52	9	3	Shildon Colliery
Manchester City	1952-53	13	3	TR
Brighton & H.A.	1954-58	175	4	TR
Queens Park Rangers	1959-60	19	3	TR

Interviewed April 1995

Ken finished his playing days at QPR under Alec Stock then went into coaching and management eventually ending his football career in 1979 after a five year spell as assistant manager at Cardiff City. He had started out at one of the country's biggest and most progressive clubs, Wolves, with amongst others Billy Wright as a team mate. Ken described his time at Molineux as "unsurpassable, a free lunch every day at Beattie's", Wolverhampton's famous department store. They boasted individually measured boots, sun-ray treatment, chiropodists and brine baths, an early example of a top club trying to give its players every possible advantage. Another high point was winning promotion to the Second Division with Brighton in 1958 adding a Third Division (South) Championship Winner's medal to his collection of memories. Jehovah took his attention from 1984 when he became a Witness based at his adopted home, Penarth in South Glamorgan. But it was golf that replaced football as his sporting passion, a game that would make anyone turn to religion. He died following a long illness shortly after our interview.

W is for Wimbledon

South-west London, strawberries and cream, Teddy Tinling, pristine whites, Henman Hill and the British triumph of hope over experience. Or do I mean South-west London, a pie and a Bovril, Sam Hammam, mud-spattered kit, The Crazy Gang and football's triumph of hope over experience.

Does any other place-name conjure up sporting images so utterly and diametrically opposed to one another? One is the epitome of the British establishment, steeped in history, playground of the rich and famous, the focus of the world for two glorious weeks each year and a club - The All England Club - that is wealthy to the point of embarrassment. The other is an anti-establishment battering ram with a mere twenty-five year history in the professional ranks, a handful of die-hard working class supporters, largely ignored by the rest of the sporting world and struggling to survive in the modern, cutthroat business that is football.

As wonderful a spectacle as tennis Wimbledon is, it is football Wimbledon that really says most about sporting endeavour. When they won the FA Cup in 1988 against the mighty Liverpool and against all the odds, they completed a journey that only eleven years earlier had seen them elected to Division Four of The Football League. By 1986 they had reached the old First Division after having been either promoted or relegated in seven of the previous seasons. The mixture of ex non-league performers and unfashionable journeyman pros

enjoyed this fairytale rise through the footballing ranks largely due to a team spirit and a common determination to defy the odds that became legendary. Their ground, Plough Lane, was an inadequate throw-back, which would never meet the requirement to become all-seater and they attracted some of the smallest crowds in the game. Yet despite all this, Wimbledon FC were able to compete and succeed as they rose through the divisions. They eventually finish sixth in The Premiership, by now 'borrowing' Selhurst Park from Crystal Palace because their own stadium didn't meet modern day standards and they couldn't afford to invest in the necessary development.

All of this is the equivalent of some bloke from Hartlepool who likes a bit of park tennis going on to compete in the Wimbledon semi-finals in a pair of cut-down jeans and a bobble hat. It took a mind-blowing victory over Pete Sampras in the previous round to eventually gain the respect of the tennis public who had been horrified by a newspaper photograph showing our hero grabbing Tim Henman's new balls at the change over. They turned out to be good friends who often went fishing together.

The sad thing about the Crazy Gang story is that, by common consent, it is not likely to happen again because of the huge gulf between the 'haves' and 'have-nots' in football. The true spirit of the underdog still occasionally surfaces in an FA Cup shock but the Wimbledon story might yet prove to be unique.

X is for Xanadu

The 'X' Team

Surprise, surprise there is no League player from the Sedgefield area whose name begins with X. In fact the only one named in my copy of the Players' Records up to 1998 is Davide Xausa, a Canadian forward who made one appearance for Stoke City in 1997. Nowadays there is the Portuguese bloke with the hair and the beard, Abel Xavier.

It could be the hit record for that skinny Antipodean chanteuse, Olivia Neutron Bomb. Or for older readers, perhaps it could rekindle memories of the Dave Dee, Dozy, Beaky, Mick and Titch 'classic' - you know, the song with the ominous cracking whip. But no, on this occasion Xanadu is the legendary city north of the modern-day Beijing where the thirteenth century Mongul hordes landed under the leadership of Kubla Khan and built the great summer palace for their gratification. It so fired the imagination of Samuel Taylor Coleridge that he was inspired to pen the classic, Kubla Khan.

In Xanadu did Kubla Khan
A stately pleasure-dome decree:
Where Alph, the sacred river, ran
Through caverns measureless to man
Down to a sunless sea

Kubla wasn't in quite the same class as his grandad, Genghis, when it came to general marauding. He was altogether more civilized, a man of letters with an eye for cultural integration. Mind you, he was no Mary Poppins and didn't exactly spend his weekends creosoting the garden fence. What strike you though are the parallels that can be drawn with the football hordes who follow their heroes like messiahs. Take Darlington, for instance. George Reynolds is the latest big time leader attempting to march on the promised land and provide his people with their own pleasure dome. And like Kubla, George has a bit of a chequered history.

Kubla Khan was the first foreigner ever to rule in China when he established himself at Cambaluc, the modern Beijing. His dominions, at this stage, stretched from Hungary to the Arctic Ocean to Korea and Asia Minor. However, it is a little known fact that the new Emperor of China also introduced chipboard kitchen surfaces to his newly acquired nation in 1271. Legend has it that he developed a very successful factory just behind the summer palace, producing kitchen tops for export. It didn't really catch on though and it was to be another 700 years before an ex safe-cracker from the North-East of England took on the world with his version of the ancient craft.

George's pleasure dome is, of course, the new 25,000 seat stadium on the outskirts of Darlington, which promises delights to match anything in European football. Had Coleridge been around today, I'm sure his epic would still have been written but in a slightly different context.

In Darlington did Kubla George
A brand new stadium decree:
Where Skerne, the sacred river, ran
Down past the JJB and then
To meet at Croft, the Tees

The 'Y' Team

	Seasons	Apps	Goals	Source
David Young (LB) Trimdon 31 January 1965 Darlington	1982-83	18	0	APP

David Young was yet another Trimdoner who found the Holy Grail and made it to the Football League. He had been an apprentice under Billy Elliot and made his League debut under the same manager on 28th December 1982 in a 1-2 defeat at Hull City who would be promoted that season. David was just one month short of his eighteenth birthday. Most of his fifteen appearances that season came at the end of the campaign and coincided with Fred Barber's arrival in goal and Darlington's best run of results. He might reasonably have expected that this would put him in a strong position for the following year. However, he played on only three further occasions in a first team shirt, two as substitute and his final game in a 1-2 defeat to local rivals, Hartlepool on Boxing Day 1983. His League career was over and he was released by Cyril Knowles at the end of the season.

David's football was strictly non-league after this with Spennymoor being his next port of call. He is still in the area, drinks in Trimdon but has recently moved to Ingleby Barwick, or as it is affectionately known to the residents therein, Spam City.

David Young from the 1982 Darlington team photo having been told to sit quietly at the front with his legs crossed.
(Photo: Darlington FC)

Y is for Yesterday

.....all my troubles seemed so far away, now it looks as though they're here to stay.

So, the good old days eh? It was so much better then than now, wasn't it?

Remember those cannonball casies, two stone heavier when wet, with laces that would leave your forehead looking like a brass rubbing? They were so much better than the modern, lightweight, scientifically tailored equivalent that can be bent and shaped by the great free-kick specialists.

Remember the maximum wage when players were routinely bought and sold without consultation and treated as the most basic of commodities? When summer wages were a fraction of winter wages and so many players found it more financially viable to play part time and hold down another job. So much better than the modern profession with all its fancy references to family security and planning for the future.

Remember the good old in-stadium clashes between warring fans? The pitched battles in the back streets and the supporters switching ends at half time in carefully calculated pincer movements to attack the away fans. So much better than today's nancy-boy, all-seater, family-orientated, customer friendly grounds where standing up is considered a crime against humanity and we are forced to watch each match in comfort.

Remember the mud bath, mid-winter playing surfaces where an intended slick pass would regularly come to a premature halt in a soupy brown puddle? Where a decent sliding tackle could take a defender from one goalmouth to the other, out of the stadium gates and down the high street - with the ball. So much better than that nasty fine turf management that so infects the modern game and leads to unnecessarily perfect football pitches in mid-January.

Remember the days when a committee would pick the England team and the manager was considered no more than a junior employee of the FA? So much better than the pretentious professionalism of the modern era where managers get to choose their own players and are appreciated as more knowledgeable than their - in football terms -amateur employers.

Remember the days when England refused to enter the World Cup? While countries like Uruguay were racking up victories the whole circus was deemed beneath us. So much better than the current desire to succeed on the world stage that has even led England to hire a foreign manager. That provides us with the opportunity to beat Argentina and Germany in a peacetime activity every four years.

Oh, I believe in yesterday!

Z is for Zealot

The 'Z' Team

And would you believe it, there is no League player from the Sedgefield area whose name begins with Z. However, there was old Worzel himself, Lee Zabek from Bristol who played 9 times for Rovers in 1997. A fine West Country name. And today there is the wonderful Gianfranco Zola. Alas, no-one from Shildon.

The big book of words on the shelf informs me that a zealot is an immoderate fanatic, usually of the religious type. For immoderate fanatic, read 'football fan'. You've all seen it. The irrational attachment to a perpetually underachieving team - Sunderland supporters will recognize this trait. The unfathomable, emotional involvement with a bunch of players who bring nothing but unhappiness, heartache and humiliation every time James Alexander Gordon recites the football results.
Mike Bateson, the Torquay chairman in 1996, was even more pointed in his description of the football fan:

"Every thousandth person created, God unhinges their heads, scoops out their brains and then issues them to a football club (as supporters)." Clearly a man with the utmost respect for the people who pay his wages.

A recent example of this type of zealot was the fat bloke sitting behind me at the recent Sunderland v Manchester United match at the Stadium of Light. He spent the game 'hollering' at the Man. U. fans to "sit down". For all he knew, there could have been twenty-two women from the WI out there baking cakes to raise money for the local scout troupe.

But being a zealous fan is like that. It's hard to comprehend. Attila the Stockbroker, the poet and Brighton supporter was equally flummoxed in 1995:

"Trying to explain why we hate Palace is like trying to explain why grass is green and vomit is lumpy. We just do."

We're used to this kind of behaviour in Britain but the Chinese find it rather more difficult to deal with. The editorial of the People's Daily of China issued this warning during the 1994 World Cup finals:

"Keep the television down low. When you see a great goal, keep your emotions under control. Don't shout loudly or applaud. You must especially guard against accidents happening because of lack of sleep."

Good advice, I'm sure you'll agree. China clearly is no place for zealots of the football kind.

But why do people become football zealots in the first place? Well, perhaps Frank Skinner has the answer:

"It says on my birth certificate that I was born in the borough of West Bromwich, in the district of West Bromwich. I said all right, all right, I'll support the bloody Albion - there's no need to twist my arm."

Records and Facts

Our 72 players have performed for 75 different teams:

Darlington	27	Barnsley	1
Hartlepool	17	Peterborough	1
Middlesbrough	9	Barrow	1
York City	6	Northampton Town	1
Bradford City	5	Arsenal	1
Sunderland	4	Tottenham Hotspur	1
Newcastle United	4	Crewe Alexander	1
Carlisle United	4	Cambridge United	1
Oldham Athletic	3	Notts Forest	1
Southend United	3	Aston Villa	1
Chester City	3	Derby County	1
Sheffield United	3	Newport County	1
Workington Town	3	Leeds United	1
Brighton and HA	3	QPR	1
Millwall	3	Manchester City	1
Walsall	2	Scunthorpe United	1
Blackpool	2	Leyton Orient	1
Colchester United	2	Luton Town	1
Ipswich Town	2	Charlton Athletic	1
Birmingham City	2	Leicester City	1
Norwich City	2	Bristol City	1
Bradford Park Avenue	2	West Bromwich A	1
Southampton	2	Halifax Town	1
Blackburn Rovers	2	Northampton Town	1
Wolverhampton W	2	Barnet	1
Lincoln City	2	Scarborough	1
Preston North End	2	Coventry City	1
Notts County	2	Stockport County	1
Hull City	2	Burnley	1
Aldershot	2	Crystal Palace	1
Chesterfield	2	Bolton Wanderers	1
Doncaster Rovers	2	Grimsby Town	1
Stoke City	2	New Brighton	1
Chelsea	2	Fulham	1
Mansfield	1	Huddersfield Town	1
Everton	1	Oxford United	1
Rochdale	1	Swindon Town	1
		Shrewsbury Town	1

Full International Caps

Gordon Cowans	England	10
Aiden Davison	Northern Ireland	3
Colin Cooper	England	2
Eric Gates	England	2

Most League Appearances up to end 2000/01 season:

Gordon Cowans	594
Gordon Jones	547
Colin Cooper	530
David Hockaday	519
Eric Gates	515
Irving Nattrass	429
Malcolm Dawes	409
Fred Barber	385
Charlie Wayman	382
Keith Nobbs	368

Most Goals up to end 2000/01 season:

Charlie Wayman	254
Eric Gates	124
Fred Richardson	66
Brian Conlon	62
Gordon Cowans	51
Michael Laverick	46
Frank Kirkup	46
Stan Cummins	45
Colin Cooper	35
David Hockaday	33

Best Strike rate (at least 10 games):

	Games	Goals	% strike rate
Charlie Wayman	382	254	66.49%
Billy Bushby	42	13	30.95%
Bobby Laverick	96	26	27.08%
Fred Richardson	244	66	27.05%
Ken Chaytor	77	20	25.97%
Brian Conlon	252	62	24.60%
Eric Gates	515	124	24.07%
Stan Cummins	222	45	20.27%
Gary Haire	77	15	19.48%
Frank Kirkup	25	46	18.18%

Youngest League debutants:

Dale Anderson	16 yrs 254 days
Peter Carr	16 yrs 259 days
John Hope	16 yrs 265 days
Ken Chaytor	16 yrs 339 days
Bill Gates	16 yrs 349 days

Oldest League debutants:

George Outhwaite	27 yrs 302 days
Joseph Roddom	26 yrs 97 days
Charlie Wayman	24 yrs
Jack Vitty	24 yrs
Frank Wayman	24 yrs

Who were the golfing ex-footballers on page 40?

Left to right: **Bill Gates, Ray Yeoman, Derek Downing, Alan Peacock, Derek McClean, Eric McMordie, George Hardwick, Frank Spraggon, Gordon Jones, Don Burlureaux, Derek Stonehouse, Johnny Spuhler, John Craggs.**